'NOTIFY ALEC RATTRAY . . .'

For Mike, Duncan, Nick, Lizzie and Hannah –
thank you all for making this book with me

'Notify Alec Rattray . . .'

A story of survival 1941–43

Written by **Meg Parkes**
from the personal papers of a
Scottish prisoner of war in the Far East

Charlie Heywood,
Meg Parkes
15.2.02

A **KRANJI** PUBLICATION

KRANJI Publications
'Kranji', 34 Queens Road, Hoylake, Wirral CH47 2AJ
Website: www.kranji.co.uk

First published 2002

British Library Cataloguing in Publication Data

Parkes, Meg
     'Notify Alec Rattray . . .'
     1st ed.
     A story of survival. Written from the
     personal papers of a Scottish prisoner of
     war in Japan 1941–1943

ISBN: 0-9541428-0-2

Designed and typeset by Kenneth Burnley, Wirral, Cheshire.
Cover designed by Nick Parkes.
Printed and bound in Great Britain by TJ International Ltd, Padstow, Cornwall.

Contents

Cover: Background map by kind permission of the British Red Cross (see p. 90)

Foreword

This remarkable wartime story tells of the privations and emotions of an officer of the 2nd Battalion of The Argyll and Sutherland Highlanders fighting, and then in captivity in Java and Japan during the period 1941 to 1943. It also poignantly shows that those who fight, are taken prisoner or who die in war are not the only ones to suffer.

The story of Atholl Duncan, and his fiancée and later wife Elizabeth Glassey, is assembled here from their own and other contemporary records. Sadly I never met Atholl, who was clearly a remarkable man. That he survived captivity by the Japanese is a testament in itself to his strength of mind and body, probably aided by, in relative terms, some good fortune. His daughter, Meg Parkes, shows that Elizabeth and other members of his family also endured imprisonment, of a different but no less painful kind, as they waited for news of him.

Atholl Duncan had an extraordinary war, in that as a member of the British Expeditionary Force he was evacuated not once, but twice, from France in 1940. He had fortunately left Singapore before it fell to the Japanese in early 1942, only to be captured in Java later in the same year.

The exploits of the Argyll and Sutherland Highlanders in Malaya and Singapore are well documented and known both within and beyond the Regimental family. This book clearly shows the human tale behind one member of that brave Battalion. We can all reflect, as Meg states in her Introduction, on the sacrifices of hundreds and thousands of such men and women, and in so doing hope and pray that such events shall never happen again.

ALASTAIR CAMPBELL
Stirling Castle
13th December 2001

Introduction

This story is about a prisoner of war experience in Java and Japan during the years from 1941 to 1943. It concerns a young man and woman and their separate and shared struggle to survive so that they might one day live out a full and good life together. It is Dr and Mrs Duncan's wartime story.

It is not solely a narrative but also a visual record of experiences, drawn from the vast array of correspondence, photographs, illustrations, maps and other documents which were collected and preserved over those long and, at times, terrifying years. As a collection the archive is unique: it is as diverse as it is remarkable.

Hidden away until the day of his liberation, the notebooks documented the story of how Atholl, a young Scottish soldier, survived his ordeal. In order to set the diaries in context and to share this piece of social history, the book also tells the story of his fiancée Elizabeth and his family back home in Britain. Theirs was a different type of 'captivity', that which was experienced by relatives, out of touch with their loved ones, worn out by fear, anxiety and the relentless grind of wartime life. Without Elizabeth in his life, it is quite possible that he might not have coped with the ordeal; thoughts and plans for their future together kept him going.

And who was Alec Rattray? He was an old school friend of Atholl's father, who had emigrated to the United States in 1924 and settled in California. Alec received a coded radio message about Atholl which was the first direct news anyone had had from him in almost two years. The original recording is just one of many artefacts which make up the collection.

The diaries were written to, and not in. He 'spoke' to the pages about day-to-day life, the joys and irritations, boredom and despair. They were intended to be read, being 'secret' only in that they were hidden from the Japanese. The very act of hiding them, the secrecy and planning involved in getting the better of the enemy, probably helped him too. What is clear is that he wanted the contents to be read and what's more he believed that they would be. Together with the letters and other documents it is an inspiring account of a period in history and of the will to survive against all the odds.

Over the years of my adult life, as the second of their four daughters, I have come to learn much about each of my parents as individuals. As a child I had no cognisance of a world before I had existed and I grew up accepting, without question, my life and family as just 'normal'. For me, therefore, it was normal that whenever the words 'Japanese' or 'Japan' were mentioned, my father would erupt in a fit of rage, exploding his feelings towards that race and their country in the general direction of the person who had uttered the words. He could be very frightening. As a teenager I found this behaviour, more often than not, just embarrassing. My reaction was to dismiss these outbursts as 'intolerant' or 'biased' with all the confidence, and ignorance, of youth. On such occasions, my mother would try to make us realise that he had had good cause.

I remember mealtimes as very tense affairs. Like his father before him, Dad was strict, insisting upon correct table manners at all times: 'Don't speak with your mouth full', 'Stop making noises when you are eating', were orders snapped at us daily. No allowances were made for youth or coughs and colds. Even friends (young and old) when visiting could get a sidelong look from Dad, or worse still, a sharp intake of breath between gritted teeth if they happened to be a noisy eater. It wasn't easy to please (and I wanted to please most of the time which is more than could be said of others round the table). Challenges to his authority became something of an art form in our household with Mum always 'piggy in the middle', trying to keep the peace, and a sense of proportion, while not undermining his authority in front of us. In private, I'm quite sure she wasn't so diplomatic. Looking back now with the benefit of hindsight I can see where much of his intolerance might have come from.

I grew up feeling that I and my sisters were loved and cherished, sharing a secure and, by and large, happy home; we didn't want for the essentials. There was humour and wit, though often with a sarcastic edge to it. But it was tense, and at the time I never really knew why.

I was in my early twenties and had been married a couple of years before I started to ask questions about their early days, curious to understand them as another married couple and not just my parents. Up until then, the war to me had been something I had pieced together throughout my childhood from conversations at home; a schoolmistress whose 'pyschotic' behaviour in class was excused and explained by premature widowhood; watching Sunday afternoon war films on TV, stretched out on the morning room floor in front of the fire; and the music, the Big Band sound of Glenn Miller (one of Dad's favourites) and the soundtrack of 'South Pacific' which I knew off by heart long before I ever saw the film. I can still remember what a revelation it was to discover that it was a war film, I'd had absolutely no idea.

As I began to identify with those years through my parents' experiences I pieced together 'their' wartime and put real people in it. Suddenly it all seemed a lot closer. It was then that I first read his diary; the large, bound, black-clothed book, 'Diary of a POW' which had sat on the morning room bookshelves throughout my childhood. Over a couple of weeks I read about what he had gone through and survived; it was both fascinating and appalling to read and I couldn't put it down. After I had given it back to him he tried to explain things so that I could better understand, but he seldom if ever initiated the subject.

I asked him how had the book been written? Had he typed up the account from memory on his return home? He told me that the diary had been handwritten in notebooks. I had never seen them before: nine notebooks large and small, one of which was home-made, bound together by bits of mosquito netting glued back and front to hold the tissue paper booklets together. His easily-legible hand formed the story in blue or black ink, whichever could be scrounged from the guards or stolen by fellow prisoners working in the offices. On looking through them something puzzled me: why had he stuck bits of blue tissue paper over some of the passages, obliterating a line, a sentence or even a paragraph here and there throughout the notebooks? He told me that it was done by his father when he was having the bound edition made.

'What? Do you mean that Grandad edited your diary?' I asked, incredulous.

I simply couldn't believe that anyone would feel they had the right to do such a thing.

'Och, well Maggie,' he said. 'I didn't care what he did, I wanted nothing to do with it. Dad was only trying to protect me I suppose, in case it was ever published. It didn't bother me.'

True. Some of the edited extracts were defamatory and could well have been libellous but even so I discovered as I read and re-read the diary that much of the editing was done to satisfy a Victorian patriarch's sense of the decent. In reality, Grandad took much of the guts out of the story and I vowed then to transcribe the whole thing again and this time it would be verbatim. So, in my late twenties I began the task, at first typing and later word processing my way through each book. It was very slow going, what with small children and life in general, but I didn't have a sense of hurry I just knew I would get it done.

When I started asking Mum questions about her experiences as a newly qualified doctor and discovered that she had not escaped either. She had had to shoulder enormous responsibility for which she simply wasn't prepared, performing operations without sufficient training because despite being young and inexperienced, she was often the most senior doctor on duty. She loved obstetrics, but no matter how much she enjoyed her work she could never relax because Atholl was so far away and in constant danger, his whereabouts unknown. Then, once the interminable waiting for news was over, and she could write to him again, communications were so unreliable. She told me that as the war dragged on she began to dread what the future might hold, fearing his return, not knowing how damaged he would be or even if she would be able to help him. The only thing she knew with absolute certainty was that she had no option but to wait for him.

In the event, when he did return home, my mother was amazed at his sheer determination to get back into life and to move forward. In those early years it was she who suffered a nervous breakdown, in silence and on her own; he was never aware of it. The stress of the war years took a heavy toll both emotionally and mentally; she couldn't share her anxiety, feeling that whatever she was going through, was as nothing compared with what he had endured.

During my early adulthood it became increasingly apparent that my father was in many ways re-visiting or 'dealing with' past experiences. After his release he got straight back into life as quickly as possible, getting married, re-starting university, graduating and then immersing himself in work, in order to provide a good home and upbringing for his growing family. But his past gradually caught up with him and all of us who knew him closely felt the effects of it, none of us escaped.

The diary and supporting correspondence reveals the story of a young man away at war, his fiancée and family left behind at home and how they tried to cope with the separation. Through the collection we can guess at how they managed, each with their own war. And in reading it, we can reflect on the enormous sacrifice made by hundreds of thousands of Allied servicemen and women and civilians. It is a story which bears telling, in case we who were not there but are fortunate to be here, who have not been tested as our parents and grandparents were, are ever tempted to overlook it.

Acknowledgements

In the writing of this book I have been encouraged and helped by so many people. First of all, to my husband and children who have put up with so much and helped me in countless ways, thank you so very much. To my sisters, Gill, Jen and Trish, thank you for your understanding.

I owe a special debt of gratitude to three people: Kenneth Burnley, without whose expertise, generosity and tireless endeavour, this book would not exist; Mr Roderick Suddaby, Keeper of Documents at the Imperial War Museum, for his guidance which has been invaluable: and John Baxter, an ex-prisoner of war who was in the same camp in Java as my father. He has been generous with his knowledge and has helped me to understand a great deal about those early days of their captivity.

Special thanks go to my parents' friends who have helped me during this monumental task: Pat Franklyn, Betty Langlands, George Armstrong, Pauline Borland, Sandy MacKenzie, Bruce McCulloch, Hazel Hinton, Mollie Davidson, John Roberts, George Downie, Ian Bennet, Gordon Christie, Tom Jarrett, Bob Mitchell, Frances Humphries, Duncan Joy, Margaret Stobie, Ray and Imelda Wood and Dave Smith.

To Jane Cameron and Debbie Johnson, who have both been so generous with their time, reading through early drafts, thank you; Heather Godfrey, Maddie Brook, Reginald Dursley, Jonathan Moffatt, Lesley Clarke, Phil Chinnery and Peter Dunstan, each of whom have their own special interest in seeing the personal history of those days remembered, thank you for your contributions.

My thanks to members of staff of the University of St Andrews including, Professor Douglas Dunn, for his encouragement and belief in my project; Dr Norman Reid, Cilla Jackson and Christine Gasgoine at the University Library for their assistance; Miss Ann Kettle and Dr Jamie Walker (Chaplain), for their understanding. Finally, Major (Retired) Alistair Campbell, Argyll & Sutherland Highland Regiment, for his help in researching many details for me.

Permissions

I am grateful to the University of St Andrews for permission to reproduce both the university and OTC crests: to the Republic of Singapore Flying Club for use of their 1940s crest; the Argyll & Sutherland Highland Regiment for use of the regimental badge; the *Straits Times* for permission to use photographs on pages 42 and 48; the British Red Cross for use of the map on page 90 and the cover. Maps on front and back flaps have been adapted from *The Emperor's Guest* by Sir John Fletcher-Cooke, published by Hutchinson. Reprinted by permission of The Random House Group Ltd.

A portion of the proceeds from the sale of this book

will be donated to further the work of the British Red Cross

Chapter 1

T.S.F. and Surrender: Coded Messages

London 1998

'I can work out most of these abbreviations, but this last one has really stumped me,' I said. 'T.S.F.? It appears a lot in the Java notebook but I can't work out what it means.'

I was sitting in the office of the Keeper of Documents at the Imperial War Museum in Lambeth. It was 1998, a lovely April morning, and from his window three floors up I could see London at work. Mr Suddaby looked at the transcript of Captain Duncan's diary once again and reflected.

Java 1942

Diary extract
8th March–12th April

8th March   *Dutch and British capitulation. Were at the tea estate between Tjikajang and coast. Made tracks for coast (Pameungpeuk) that evening with Des. Met D, G, M-C and Pace en route.*

9th March   *Reached coast. No boats, had bathe and discussed position.*

Heard Blenheim had left aerodrome that morning for Australia. Curtiss Hawk with aileron damaged left on aerodrome. Phoned EL. Slept on beach at night. Many rumours about boats coming to our rescue – all false. RAF origin.

10th March   *Frank Knight, Pat, Dutch, Allan arrived at P. Shifted up to the observation post. Many rats and land crabs.*

11th–17th March *Still at beach. Killed 5½ ft. cobra on beach.*

18th March   *Returned to GHQ at T'jang.*

19th March   *Left for Tjibatoe by road. Saw first Japs at Garoet. Billeted on FW Winter.*

25th March   *The great binge after return from Bandoeng as ADC to Sitwell saw EL.*

27th March   *Entrained for Batavia. Felt very ill for past 3 days. Natives hostile en route. Dutch OK Andir badly smashed by bombing. Crated yank planes seen in siding. Left T 0630, arrived TP 1930. Collapsed on platform with malaria. Car to camp.*

> 28th March   *Feeling rotten. Had camera and mattress pinched. Doc can only give me quinine.*
>
> 30th March   *Better today. Moved in camp with M-C, Des, Glasgow & Day. Start of great rations ramp (sic)*
>
> 31st March–12th April   *Rice main diet. Much discontent due to RASC adopting FYJ policy. All surplus rations handed back on 11th. All feeling very bolshie. (NB: FYJ – f— you Joe)*
>
> 12th April   *First bathing parade today: not very pleasant due to marine insect activity. T.S.F. better last night.*

After a moment he continued,

'Yes, this is quite a puzzle. I'm not sure what the initials T.S.F. refer to but, from the context it appears in and the fact that it appears frequently, I would guess it could be a secret radio. Though what the initials refer to, I can't say. Sorry not to be more help.'

He continued looking through the photocopies of documents that had been acquired, hidden away and then gathered together to bring home all those years ago. Looking up he said,

'You know, one of the things that sets your father's diary apart from others of its type are the detailed plans of the camps and the lists of names in his notebooks. It was unusual for prisoners to make detailed drawings of their surroundings and these are very good. But it is rare to see such full details of other prisoners: lists of names and addresses like this can be very useful.'

How interesting. By now I was so familiar with this material but I had no experience of other accounts with which to compare. The few books I'd read were diaries or accounts written by people known to Dad, prisoners in one or more of the camps that he'd been in, and so their stories were of particular interest to him.

'And one other thing,' said Mr Suddaby, 'that story of the prisoners in Java using homing pigeons, now that I've never heard before. That's new. There are two references to it and it's very interesting. You do occasionally read about prisoners of war keeping animals as pets in this way. Yes, this certainly is a remarkable collection and thank you for lodging a transcript with the museum.'

I thanked him for his time and for his help. Just before I got up to leave I returned to the initials:

'It makes sense if, as you say, the 'N.B.G.' and the 'V.G.' mean 'no bloody good' or 'very good'. And if it was a radio they would have had to refer to it in code in case the Japs got wind of it. He was after all a cipher officer so using codes would be second nature to him. I wish I'd asked him; never mind, it's too late now.'

On the train back home to Wirral I had time to think and my mind wandered back to the year before and their final weeks. So, 1997 was the year that we wouldn't forget. I had often tried to face the inevitability of life without my parents by wondering when would I have to face it? What year would I come to dread remembering? Where? Who first? What then? Always questions, but I didn't want to know the answers. I couldn't share it at the time, though now I recognise it as a type of anxiety state that many people experience. For me it was like a shield, a way of preparing myself. Like my mother I'm a 'coper', and like her I worry about bridges that need crossing, situations and problems that are often so far ahead of me but, 'if I sort them out now', I reason, maybe I can work out strategies which will enable me to cope. But life has a habit of not always working out the way we expect. What unfolded over the Christmas and New Year of 1996/7 and what it would leave in its wake, I could never have envisaged not even in my worst nightmare.

Dad's illness crept up on us insidiously, being masked by his irascible and self-sufficient character. And perhaps also, by fear. Both of them possessed an instinctive understanding of how to help others and throughout their working life in medicine had touched many lives for the better. But when it came to their own ill-health they knew too much, they couldn't be protected. In December 1996 he knew he was dying and he chose to deal with it by not discussing it. We knew too, because the doctors had told us, but everyone respected his wishes; he didn't want to talk about it, so we didn't. Inevitably this put an almost unbearable strain on Mum who was far from well herself.

He began to use that precious time to 'hand over', wanting to discuss how I was progressing with transcribing the diaries, to be sure that I understood as much as possible. But time was running out and many things were left unexplained, for instance those initials, T.S.F. . . .

A few days after the meeting at the Imperial War Museum, I was talking to a friend of mine who taught French at the girls' Grammar School nearby. Elspeth is a Scot too, and I always enjoy her company. She was interested in my quest to find out what the initials had meant and she listened patiently as I recounted what Mr Suddaby had said about it possibly being reference to a radio in the camp. Intrigued she pondered,

'Tell me again, what were the initials?'

'T - S - F - V - G: something, something, something, very good,' I repeated.

'T.S.F. – telegrafie sans fils; it's French for "wireless", could that be it?' Elspeth asked.

Of course. The relief. The glorious sense of relief. Mystery solved. He was a cipher officer, he was experienced in using codes, he'd been in France on active service in 1940 and, as I had recently discovered when reading his Java diary notes, he had taught rudimentary French to some of the other prisoners. He was determined from the outset of his captivity to record events, irrespective of the threats of punishment and so he needed codes in case his notebook was found. No, it had to be the answer, I couldn't see any other explanation making more sense. And what better way for me to make the connection than from a fellow Scot! Later, when I suggested this explanation to Mr Suddaby he agreed that it seemed the most likely interpretation.

Going back to his time in Java following the Dutch capitulation, he kept both brief notes and later a narrative of his adventures during the time that he referred to as 'the lull'. The following extract paints a vivid picture:

1942

On the evening of Feb. 24th 1942, chaos reigned in the headquarters of the SWPC (South West Pacific Command), as the majority of its members were leaving Lembang en route for Tjilatjap by road on the following morning at 4am. Files were being burned, documents and equipment packed, officers were trying to get their effects together, arms and ammunition were being issued and, of course, the usual orders, counter orders and disorder. Lieut. Des Campion and self maintained an aloof air to all this, as on the previous evening we had volunteered to stay behind, but nevertheless, deep down, felt rather envious and wondered exactly what the future held for us. As was only natural and fitting on such occasions, the bar receipts soared, and I still bear evidence in the form of a scarred finger of that evening's frolics. Having tired of watching other people work, Des said to me, 'Let's go over to the sergeants' mess and bid them goodbye,' whereupon we retired from circulation for the next two hours and worked up a fine appetite for dinner. After the meal we continued our rounds, our progress through the camp being all too easily marked by sundry bangs, thumps and songs, culminating in the crash of breaking glass, which cut short a rather indifferent rendering of 'Ten Green Bottles'.

The final farewell at 4am next morning was definitely a subdued affair and when all the vehicles had departed, Des and I returned to bed.

After a belated breakfast in the strangely silent dining room, a final sort-out of kit took place, and I discovered to my horror that some bright individual had removed a small case containing all my tropical kit when my big trunk was loaded onto the lorry, and all that I possessed in the way of clothes was one soiled outfit that I had been wearing the previous evening. Happily, Des was able to provide me with shirts and shorts but nevertheless I felt very annoyed over the loss of these clothes.

Later when my car (bought for one guilder) had been loaded with stores, kit and tommy gun we departed from Lembang to take up our duties under General Sitwell. The few peaceful remaining days were a Godsend after the hectic time we had experienced at Lembang. It was here that we discovered 'George', the most cheerful servant we had come across in our sojourn in the Far East; his inevitable toothy smile on all occasions, good or bad, provided a welcome relief from the usual run of surly natives, and afforded us a great deal of amusement.

Mention has been made of a one guilder car and I think this is worthy of a short description as it proved a valuable and faithful friend right up to the last. When General Pownall's staff left Singapore on HMS 'Anking' this car, belonging to one of the officers was brought along, it being a green 10 HP Standard saloon which rattled fiercely and possessed the most temperamental brakes I have ever known. The springs could practically have been used as a straight edge, whilst an anaemic horn and loose steering added interest – and sometimes excitement – to driving. With all these shortcomings and no attention whatsoever, she carried us and a superabundance of junk for more than 2,000 miles over some of the worst roads it has ever been my misfortune to drive, accepting anything from pool petrol to 100 octane aviation spirit without protest.'

One of the most fascinating artefacts in his collection is another message, this being one that Dad had decoded himself. First of all it is helpful to understand the changing chain of command during the turbulent period between December 1941 and the end of February 1942. It was recorded by Dad at the beginning of the bound copy of the diary:

At the time of General Wavell's appointment as Supreme Commander in Chief of Allied Forces in the South West Pacific, Capt. Duncan was a member of the staff of General Pownall who, up to that time had himself been Commander-in-Chief Far East. This staff was transferred en bloc to General Wavell who established his headquarters at Lembang, a small village just north of Bandoeng in the mountains of Java, where it remained until February 25th, 1942 when it was dissolved. A small portion of the HQ staff remained behind in Java to command the remaining British Forces who were placed under the command of General Sitwell, who in turn was under the Dutch Commander-in-Chief, General Ter Poorten. (For a brief time latterly, Capt. Duncan was ADC to General Sitwell).'

He told me one evening in December 1996 the story of how he came to have a copy of a secret decoded message:

'During late February 1942, I was the cipher officer on duty when, in the early hours of the morning, an urgent message came through for General Sitwell from Dutch HQ.

'Having decoded the message, I handed it to the stenographer to type up with the instruction, "Shove in an extra carbon, I want a copy of this," as I realised all too clearly what it meant. This was notice of the conditions of the surrender that had been sent out to "Black Force" – Allied HQ on Java.

'Once typed I took it straight away and woke General Sitwell.

'"Any message, Sir?"

'"No, that will be all, Duncan."

'That copy spent the next three and a half years folded up and concealed inside the lining of my Glengarry.' (A Glengarry is the woollen cap worn by the Argylls.)

He was holding the folder which contained within its plastic sleeves the terms of surrender. It was his small piece of world history and he treasured it. The message is shown opposite (for ease of display the pages have been merged into one).

Surrender. First Singapore and then Java. Captain Duncan and a group of fellow officers had no intention of following these instructions and they spent the best part of the following three weeks trying to find some way to escape. The diary entries for 8–27 March at the beginning of the chapter document that fruitless search. As the net began to tighten the narrative continued,

Opposite:
De-coded message notifying General Sitwell of the terms of the surrender of Allied Forces on Java, February 1942.

1942

It might be as well, at this point, to give a brief description of the general conditions under which the British troops were living immediately following the capitulation. The northern side of the island of Java, is for the main part flat, abounding in mangrove swamps and padi fields, this region stretching back from the coast of the Java Sea to the foothills thirty miles away, whilst the Java Sea itself is shallow and calm with the result that all fishing is carried out on this coast. On the other hand, the south coast is bounded by the Indian Ocean which on occasion is very rough and always has a tremendous surf line, the mountains running right down to the sea. This explains the absence of boats on the south coast. From Tjikajang to Pameungpeuk the road runs through wild country, jungle forests stretching for miles on each side of the road whilst only a few native kampongs are to be found along the whole fifty odd miles. The country further to the west is equally wild, the natives in that area being definitely hostile and would not

R.A.F. Form 9.
S 575 (Naval)

MESSAGE FORM.

Office Serial No.................

Call   IN

and:—

Preface OUT

| | No. of Groups GR | Office Date Stamp. |

(Above this line is for Signals use only)

TO*

    BLACKFORCE   16 AA BDE

FROM*   GHQ

| Originator's Number | Date 9 | In Reply to Number and Date |

Following are terms of surrender accepted by C in C RNI Army and will be carried
out forthwith (.) 1 (.) Unconditional surrender (.) 2 (.) All hostilities
must immediately cease (.) 3 (.) Hoist white flag as sign of capitulation (.)
4 (.) All troops to be immediately disarmed and assembled for surrender (.)
Troops in defended positions or fortifications after disarming to be assembled
in a clearly visible space (.) Remaining troops to be assembled in camps or
barracks with their arms and ammunition to be piled together and placed under
guard (.) 5 (.) The above four conditions must be completed by midday 9th
March (.) 6 (.) Bodies of dead or wounded Japanese soldiers and their equipment
and all other Japanese property to be surrendered as soon as possible (.) 7 (.)
All demolition not only of war materials arms ammunition etc but also ground means
of transport buildings etc is forbidden (.) 8 (.) Communication with abroad is
forbidden (.) 9 (.) Movements of Japanese troops will be continued (.) 10 (.)
For the maintenance of law and order armed guards are to be provided and supplied
with limited arms and ammunition (.) As far as possible these should be under
command of a responsible officer (.) These guards should also be provided with
a white arm band and white flag (.) 11 (.) To give effect to the above terms
units will immediately act as follows (:) (a) No further moves will take place(.)
(b) Units will report their locations including those of sub units separated
from their parent unit (.) (c) Troops will be assembled in open spaces
along the road under unit officers and NCOs (.) (d) Arms will be piled under
armed guard wearing white arm bands (.) (e) Unit HQs will fly a white flag (.)
GHQ will be moving from present location about G of LIMBOANG to TJIKADJANG
in two echelons (.) Car party at 1030 hrs (.) Lorry party at 1300hrs (.)
Roads must be kept clear for this move (.)

hesitate to attack and kill white men with their 'parangs' – a long knife rather like a butchers cleaver – just for the few clothes they wore or for their watch or rings. Many of the survivors of the cruisers Houston and Perth which had been sunk in the Sundra Straits, reached the shores of Java only to be butchered by these murderous Bantams, as they are called. As word of the capitulation got round, the entire allied force, excluding the Dutch, concentrated about this road with the result that its entire length was dotted with small communities, each with its own meagre stock of tinned rations, sleeping accommodation varying from lorries to home made shelters constructed out of bamboo and banana leaves, whilst drinking and ablution water was drawn from nearby streams, this being an extremely dangerous practice in tropical countries where dysentry and typhoid are rife. As the whole of the south coast area is a notorious fever district, and as the majority of the men had no anti-malarial equipment, this having been lost or jettisoned, the anxiety of the medical authorities can well be imagined. Our particular community lived in comparative luxury, being housed in KPM godowns whilst we ourselves lived in what had been a Dutch look out post which was situated on a small knoll close by the beach. To reach our eyrie, it was necessary to cross a river over which a single track railway line was carried by a rickety wooden bridge and on gazing into the river from this, a variety of warlike stores ranging from smashed rifles to motor cycles and wireless sets could be seen lying on the mud bed. The path which led to our abode consisted of steps hewn out of the rock, whilst halfway up a large tomb – a constant source of worry to Des at night – lent an air of mystery to the place; as for our billet itself, although not luxurious, was certainly a cut above the usual run of things as it was an attap hut divided into two, this being used as sleeping quarters whilst the nearby air-raid shelter served as a kitchen, our dining room being of the open air variety. On our first night Des and I slept in the car, expecting to be rounded up by the Japs the following morning, but next day, as none were forthcoming, an attempt was made to get some semblance of organisation in the community to eke out our rations as long as possible, our own particular supply having been obtained from an abandoned three ton lorry which had been ditched not far from GHQ and which was loaded to capacity with tinned goods . . .

'On the second day of our stay at Pameungpeuk six very footsore and weary individuals arrived at the godown complete with natives acting as bearers. This party turned out to be Flight Lieut. Knight, ACI Cheeked, Pte. Martin and Vandervoord both of the AIF or Frank, Pat, Allan, and Dutch and two others whose names I have now forgotten. They had just completed a 70 mile trek through the jungle and along the beach and were all in when they reached us, whilst one of their number was suffering from malaria and *had to be taken off to hospital that evening. As we were just brewing our afternoon tea, we invited them to join us, this offer being readily accepted so seated around the car, we swapped news and discussed plans for the future as we felt it would be better to join another escape party than to try and make a break on our own. Frank broke the news to us that there were no boats at all along the stretch of beach that he had covered and that it would be suicide to try and lie up in the foothills as the natives were very unfriendly and even if they did not slaughter you out of hand as they were Mohamedans who believe that to kill a white man ensures your entry into paradise in the next world, they would most likely turn you over to the Japs to collect the price that had been put on our heads by the Japanese. During the whole of that day a steady stream of callers arrived to partake of the particularly fine bathing facilities offered by this part of the beach and indeed such was the case during the whole of our stay at the south coast. That evening up at our 'home from home' Frank asked if we would be willing to throw in our lot with him as two members of his party had dropped out, his plan being to head along the beach to Tjilatjap where it was hoped that we would be able to buy or steal a boat capable of making the trip to Australia. In view of their exhausted condition it was decided to spend the next few days at Pameungpeuk but as our rations were running low, I should return to GHQ to glean news and obtain more foodstuffs. On the following day we had a visit from Col. Russell of GHQ who informed us of special terms that had been granted to the British troops by the Japanese which were roughly as follows:*

(1) The entire British forces were to be concentrated between Garoet and six miles from the sea and would ultimately be employed on tea estates, there being no question of being put behind barbed wire.

(2) Our own people were to be responsible for administration and provisioning.

(3) All war stores to be handed over intact, as small proportion of transport to be allotted to us for the maintenance of essential services.

(4) All personnel to wear a white arm band.

(5) We would be permitted to write two letters per month and receive any incoming mail.

(6) Anyone attempting to escape would be shot.

As Col. Russell pointed out, these terms provided they were kept, were extremely generous, as our surrender had been unconditional and the Dutch forces were already behind barbed wire and urged that we return to our respective units to facilitate administration. This gave us a great deal of food for thought as we had never, in our wildest dreams, imagined terms like these, but the general concensus of opinion was that the Japs were playing a deep game though we could not see what the catch was, so decided to continue with our original plan; accordingly I paid a visit to GHQ on the following day, where, to my amazement, instead of being ordered to return to the fold, was offered the job of acting as a lookout in case anything should arrive at Pameungpeuk and a suitable code was arranged but I made it quite clear that should anything come in, I would inform them of it but depart immediately I had discharged that duty. As to where Japanese troops were located, they could give me no information as up to that time the only people at GHQ who had seen a Jap were the General and Air Vice Marshal who journeyed daily to Bandoeng to confer with them so having been given a lunch in no way comparable to those I had at the coast and carrying a chit to the OC RASC dump at Tjisompet authorising me to draw ample rations I set out on the return journey. On arriving back I found the party discussing whether to make a break for it there and then as an order had come round that everybody had to return to their unit so broke the news that we had been officially appointed as a piquet post for rounding up stragglers and would be assured of rations whenever the need arose, whereupon it was decided to remain where we were and await developments. Time quickly passed as our days were spent in bathing, fishing and shopping expeditions to the village where we haggled with natives over the prices of chickens, sugar, eggs, fruit and sarongs . . .'

Eventually they had to give themselves up and their next stop was Tandjong Priok, a notorious fever spot on the outskirts of Batavia. This large dock-lined basin was their destination at the end of the long and tedious rail journey from Tjilatjap. Captain Duncan together with a few others who were sick were lucky, as the Japs in charge of the transfer provided trucks to take them into the camp.

Tandjong Priok was also the name given to the large, multinational, transit camp that they were herded into. Pre-war the area had been home to the native dock labourers who occupied the squalid and inadequately built huts on the dockside.

The different nationalities – British, American, Dutch, Australian, as well as a few civilians – occupied separate sub-camps within the main camp. Prisoners were required to form working parties to do manual work on the docks, shifting supplies for the Japs and clearing bomb damage. According to convention, officers were not meant to work, their role being to organise these groups, keep order and discipline and accompany their men on the working parties. One reason for this division of labour was that the

Tandjong-Priok.
Hangars.

Japanese were simply overwhelmed with the numbers of prisoners they had taken. They had not expected to take prisoners for it was unthinkable to the Japanese psyche to surrender, fighting to the death being the only honourable alternative to victory. The victors now found themselves having to cope with tens of thousands of Allied personnel. It was expedient that they relied on the Allied officers to keep order and it was in everyone's interest that a sense of order was quickly established and adhered to.

Captain Duncan, along with all those who had survived so far, was to spend the next few months as a prisoner in Tandjong Priok. For him it would be eight formative months.

The dockside where the men worked. Tandjong Priok camp was situated to the far left of photo, behind trees – a prewar postcard, one of a collection found by the author in the mid-1980s.

Chapter 2

Boy Meets Girl

Andrew Atholl Duncan was born on 4 March 1918 in the mediaeval university town of St Andrews in the Kingdom of Fife. Though commonly referred to as a town St Andrews is technically a city (albeit a very small one) thanks to King James VI who bestowed Royal Burgh status upon the townsfolk in 1620. It is home to the oldest university in Scotland (the second oldest in Great Britain).

He was known to the family as Atholl. Born at home, he was the youngest of three children and the only son. His parents Andrew and Amelia lived with their two older daughters Nesta (aged 7) and Bunty (nearly 5) at 52 Argyle Street just outside the West Port at the far end of South Street.

His parents had married in 1910 in Stirling. Amelia Fairley was an English girl and one of nine children who came from the Jesmond Dene area of Newcastle-upon-Tyne. They had met when she was working as a children's nurse to the Laing family in Edinburgh and the young couple set up home in St Andrews. Andrew (and for a few years his brother William) worked with their father Andrew Aitken Duncan building up the family motor and cycle engineering business.

The Duncan family had originally come from St Monans, one of the once-busy fishing ports in the East Neuk of Fife along the coast from St Andrews. In the late 18th century their forebears had owned one of the whaling ships that had sailed from the port to fish the Arctic waters for this large and valuable catch. The head of the family, William Duncan, eventually had to come ashore when he lost his boat and almost 'drowned', not at sea but at the gaming tables where he frittered away much of the family's wealth. After a time working on the land, the family moved to St Andrews where they bought The Crown Inn in Abbey Street which they ran for many years. This was where Andrew

Young Andrew and Amelia.

2 St Mary's Place
St Andrews.

Aitken and his five brothers and sisters had grown up and from where he started his working life as a general labourer. Soon he was taking steps to improve his lot and after a brief sojourn as an articled clerk (which ended rather abruptly following a somewhat physical disagreement with his employer!) the young man decided the time had come to branch out on his own. He opened his first cycle business in 1896 at 130 Market Street.

The business was a thriving concern and before long had expanded to include garaging and maintenance of the new automobiles which, in those pre-war days, were becoming increasingly popular. This expansion necessitated a move further along the street to larger premises at 2 St Mary's Place, where Duncan's Garage had the distinction of operating the first petrol pump in the town. Lock-up garages were at a premium and the business capitalised on providing this facility to the growing number of novice motorists. This was a lucrative business as few of the private properties in the town had private garaging or the space for it. The expansion continued, and in 1911 an additional and larger garage was built in Argyle Street adding to the stock of garage space for private and hire cars. It was to the house which had been built beside these premises that the young family moved shortly before Atholl's birth. Situated in a pleasant area on the outskirts of the town, their home was close to the wide open space of Cockshaugh Park – a wonderful playground for the young

Young Atholl (on left) and friend outside the garage and house at 52 Argyle Street.

family – and the restful beauty of the Lade Braes walk where during the winter months Atholl's father spent much of his free time engaging in the sport of curling on the frozen ponds.

Within a generation the Duncans had become respectable members of the town and trading community and both Andrew Aitken and later his son Andrew would serve as elders of Holy Trinity Parish church in South Street for well over sixty years in all.

Father and son were also keen golfers as one might expect being natives of the 'home of golf'. They were both members of the Thistle Club, the second oldest golf club in St Andrews, founded in 1813 by members of the town's business community (the oldest is of course the Royal and Ancient founded in 1754). The younger Andrew had been a schoolboy champion and in his early adult life played off a +2 handicap. The year 1924 was auspicious as both father and son were now respectively President and Captain of the club. On his retirement the following year the president presented the A. A. Duncan Gold Medal as the prize for a bi-annual tournament to be played in Spring and Autumn each year, a tradition which continues to this day.

The arrival of a much-wanted son was heralded with great joy in the family. Atholl grew into a fine-looking lad, the apple of his father's eye and his mother's wee angel, her pet name for him being 'Apple Dumpling'. In 1923 aged 5, Atholl joined his sisters at the Madras College (also his father's old school). The preparatory school was housed in a two-storey stone building to the right of Madras College.

The school had been founded in 1833 by Dr Andrew Bell and occupied these and other distinctive buildings around a magnificent stone quadrangle either side and to the rear of the remains of Blackfriars Monastery in South Street. The school's early reputation was built around Dr Bell's belief in the Monitorial System of education which he had first seen in practice in India. It was a system whereby a relatively small number of professional teachers instructed the older pupils who in turn taught the younger ones their lessons.

Atholl enjoyed his years there taking part in all aspects of school life with enthusiasm and is remembered by one classmate as being 'always full of fun'. He was adventurous and honed his mountaineering skills by spending many a happy hour when not at school, climbing among the rafters of the new garage, a pastime guaranteed to worry his anxious mother.

From an early age he showed signs of becoming an accomplished sportsman and played football, rugby and cricket for the school. He was a strong

Extract from register.

Madras College on left and Preparatory School right.

swimmer, developing his skills during his teens by joining other fearless souls diving into the sea from the cliff face under the Scores and like most of his generation, he made great use of the Step Rock baths. But it was hardly surprising that the sport he excelled at was golf. During his teens he often played a round on the Old Course before school and became a keen competitor.

In 1934 Atholl was one of the youngest members of the Madras College

Madras golfing team with Atholl Duncan seated far right, aged 14.

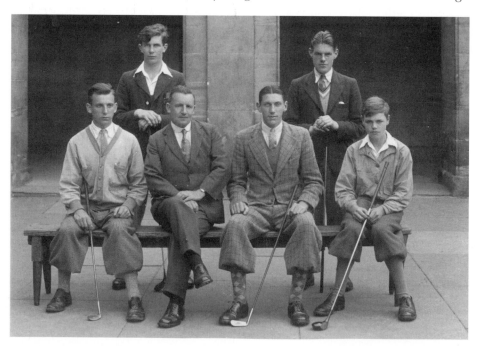

golf team and later that year was the only school boy to make it through to the final round of the Eden Tournament. This was no mean feat, as to qualify for the Eden players have to play off a handicap of 9 or under. It was a remarkable achievement for such a young lad.

Atholl, age 10, beside a de Havilland Moth, taken by his father.

Other hobbies which started young were stamp collecting, model-making and photography. In the case of the latter local influences were once again strong. The history of photography has roots in St Andrews being the hometown of Dr Thomas Rodger, a pioneer in the development of the art. To all of these interests he would give his best, a tendency carried into his adult life with almost obsessive zeal.

From very early on though his greatest passion was for flying and all things aeronautical. Atholl's love of aeroplanes was not merely that of many young boys of his time; it had been engendered from his early days when he would accompany his father to supply the fuel for visiting planes which landed and took off from the town end of the West Sands. Duncan's Garage van would arrive on the Bruce Embankment loaded with fuel cans and supply the waiting aircraft which would be surrounded by crowds of curious onlookers.

As late as 1938 visiting aeroplanes chartered by golfers would land in a field at Balgove, close to the links (this area has now become home to the sixth golf course – a nine-hole – in St Andrews).

The young lad would also regularly ride out in the van to deliver fuel cans to the newly-established Leuchars airfield which was situated five miles or so from St Andrews on the Dundee road between the paper mill at Guardbridge and the village of Leuchars. From 1911 military balloons were operated from this site and during the First World War it became a base for the Royal Flying Corps. What a shock it must have been to the inhabitants of the tiny village, wrapped around its beautiful Norman church, to realise that once established this new neighbour was not going to move on; and what a noisy neighbour it turned out to be!

During the war years Duncan's Garage continued to provide services to the RAF base which helped to ensure the business' survival through times of fuel shortages and cutbacks. A letter from B.O.A.C. who ran the base, was found among my grandfather's papers and bears testament to the importance of this connection. Vital fuel supplies would be needed to continue this support work as well as access to spare parts, both of which would be a help to other customers.

Nowadays Leuchars is an RAF Air Defence base, home to the 13

Letter from BOAC.

Tornado F3's of No. 43 Squadron and 12 Tornado F3's of No. 111 Squadron. No visit to St Andrews is complete without hearing that unique combination of sounds: the North Sea waves rolling on to the West Sands combining with the roar of Tornadoes as they take off to do endless circuits and bumps, sweeping round over Balmullo Hill and then out across the Eden estuary again and again. After many years, I still find it a strangely comforting and reassuring mix. And no holiday with our grandparents passed without the obligatory visit to RAF Leuchars where Dad would park up beside the boundary fence (no longer allowed) to watch the noisy craft going about their routine business. While he never tired of this compulsory holiday activity, his passengers were not so lucky. Poor Mum left with the four of us plus a minimum of two dogs all fighting for space on the back seat – it wasn't terrific fun. Later on we would sit through what seemed like hours (but was in all honesty only minutes) of home cine films devoted to expert panning with target dead centre and not a family member in sight.

During the late 1920s the young family moved to the outskirts of the town, to a new house which Grandad had had built. The Lea Rig was on the Grange Road and overlooked St Andrews Bay and the East Sands. It was an attractive detached villa with dormer windows and pan-tiled roof. The spacious garden must have been a joy for Amelia after years of living beside the garage and it afforded Atholl and his friends plenty of ammunition, in the form of apples, with which to take pot shots at passers-by. As he neared his teens he adding cycling to his ever-growing list of pastimes, joining friends or setting off on his own to roam the surrounding area and cycling for miles on the highways and byways through the rich, rolling landscape of east Fife.

During the mid-1930s Duncan's Garage made its final move when it sold 2 St Mary's Place to the Victoria Café and took over next door, No. 3 (which was and still is known as Mansefield) with the large area behind it being converted into more garaging and workshops. The business now comprised not only the Argyle Street garage but also additional lock-ups at Ellice Place on North Street. Following extensive alterations to the frontage of this large property, to create two shop fronts with store and workrooms behind, the family moved from the Lea Rig to take up residence at Mansefield, the fine though somewhat austere stone house which was situated just back from the street in the centre of town. I wonder what Grandma must have felt about this move and the loss of her garden.

My early memories of visits to stay with Grandma and Grandad are of this house which was entered through the front door in the centre of the building between the two shops. At the far end of the hallway, which always smelt oily, we went up a long, winding stone staircase with its fine wrought-iron banisters topped with a polished mahogany rail, to the first floor living accommodation. Just going this far was exciting as nowhere else in our

Mansefield, 3 St Mary's Place.

experience did people 'live' upstairs. The first floor had a drawing room in which I can clearly remember the tall, wooden window shutters and a long wooden curtain pole with large rings, which rattled most satisfyingly when the curtains were swished backwards and forwards. There was also a dining room, small kitchen, two bedrooms and a bathroom. We reached our attic bedrooms via a narrow wooden staircase which spiralled up and reminded us of the Square Tower steps at the cathedral, our rooms looking out to the rear over the large yard.

Atholl with Don Clark, an undergraduate friend, on South Street, both wearing their scarlet gowns.

One of my strongest memories is the day that me and my two younger sisters, Gilly and Jenny, were told off by Grandad for playing hide and seek inside the stacked rings of tyres in the back store room. I'm quite sure that we had been told repeatedly (for obvious reasons) that we mustn't play downstairs so it was no more than we deserved, but the smell of rubber combined with a sense of fear (he was cross!) remain crystal clear to me to this day.

In 1936, aged 18, Atholl entered the university following his older sister

Nesta (seven years his senior and the first member of the family to go to university), who had graduated in 1933 with a BA Hons in English. He was to study for a BSc degree in Mechanical Engineering which, given his ability and background, was an obvious choice.

At his own admission, Atholl was not the most diligent of students. There were many distractions, golf, cycling and drinking to name but three! Typical of many of the young men of his day, he was keen to join the university's OTC (Officer Training Corps) which also proved to be an absorbing and interesting diversion to his studies.

Several times a week the Drill Hall, which was opposite his grandparents home at 4 Alfred Place, had reverberated to the sounds of square bashing and drill and Atholl had quickly developed a deep dislike of this facet of military life. However, the OTC ran camps and mountaineering expeditions in the Highlands and with him, throughout these years of military training, went his camera so that he could record the events, people and places.

He was a typical undergraduate, ever ready to indulge in some good-natured tomfoolery as well as the odd

St Andrews University Mountaineering Club 1938.

Above:
Atholl on Ben Cruachan.

Below: Atholl seated far right on Ben Eunaich.

Atholl (right) and
Bill Moore – pretending
to be the worse for
wear!

bout of reckless abandon. There was the occasion one evening when, for a dare, he and several friends walked round the top of St Rule's Tower (the Square Tower and very high) in the Cathedral precincts. They then proceeded to scare the pants off passers-by on their way to and from the Harbour through the Pends, who firmly believed they had seen an apparition in the graveyard!

It was hardly surprising that the appeal of university society attracted him, having been cosseted and indulged by his mother and two older sisters and alternately spoilt and admonished by his strict, Presbyterian father. Student life was a signal to the young man to reach out and en – joy! Later on as the following extracts illustrate, studying became very important to him and he bitterly regretted the waste of time, vowing to do better in the future.

Motoyama – 11 Feb 1943 – Now that we have some money, an attempt is being made to buy some books, and I have requested information regarding textbooks in Chemistry, Physics and Maths so that I shall not lose touch altogether with these subjects.

And later still in Zentsuji he wrote:

February 28th 1944 – Making good progress with the maths these days and feel that I am really getting somewhere. It is often said that opportunity does not knock twice, but I think that this is my second chance and am not going to let it slide as I did when I went to University. To my mind, George Blakey is heaven-sent, as it means that I can get hours of individual tutoring which would have cost a small fortune anywhere other than in a POW camp.
The only drawback is that it is very difficult to concentrate in a room where about 27 others are all talking or walking about, but tho' my progress may not be meteoric, it is at least steady and I do understand all that I have covered. George says that it will take about a year to cover the 2nd BSc. course, which is just about right if my estimation of the duration of this war is correct; however, the news has been quite reassuring of late and there is a slight possibility that I may not "graduate from Zentsuji" but this will not worry me overmuch!

Not only does this indicate a certain maturity and sense of purpose (and his very Scottish instincts!) but also a deep-rooted conviction that he would return home.

He lived at home during his undergraduate years and one suspects that he lived something of a double life. Certainly he would later recall that little work was done in favour of pursuing his interests which were many and varied and now also included angling. He and his old school-friend, Robert Dickson, became regulars up at Cameron reservoir outside St Andrews, fishing for trout for hours on end from a boat on the loch. Despite the exhortations of professors and parents, in view of what his future was to hold it was perhaps no bad thing. Knowing the area so well he must have regarded it as no less than a duty to share his knowledge of most of the local hostelries with his new friends, many of whom being from south of the border, didn't know the area at all.

A Yorkshire lass

One such newcomer was Joan Elizabeth Glassey, known to her friends as Liz, from Bradford in Yorkshire. In October 1937 she arrived at 'Kinnessburn', a large Victorian, detached house in Kennedy Gardens, a quiet road to the west of the town, which served as one of the female residences of University Hall. She was one of a small number of women medical students at the university in those pre-war days.

Born on 17 November 1918 in Barrow-in-Furness, the only daughter and younger child of school teacher Stanley Churchill Glassey (SCG) and his wife Lilian, Joan was a bonny, healthy baby. Within a few months of her birth the family moved to Bradford when her father took up a teaching post at Bradford Grammar School, joining the Classics staff as an English and Latin master. This appointment signalled the flowering of her father's gifted academic career after years of perseverence and hard work. It could all have been so different had it not been for the wise words of another teacher a generation earlier.

Elizabeth the bejantine (1st year student).

Stanley Glassey was born in 1888, one of five children. The family lived in Handsworth, Birmingham. He adored his mother, Sarah, who was to all accounts a gentle, astute and diplomatic woman, but he was completely in awe of his father Charles, an Ulsterman possessed of a fiery temper. Stanley, a self-confessed 'slow starter' when it came to learning, was prone to be (in his father's company at least) rather clumsy. Charles frequently despaired of his younger son, and, gave up all hope of him ever achieving anything, saying that he would only be good for the army or the clergy! However, thanks to the timely praise of one of his teachers, young Stanley gained in confidence and found his way into a lifetime of learning and teaching. SCG described the defining incident in an interview with Ian Hargreaves, the *Telegraph & Argus*' correspondent (Bradford's evening newspaper) in May 1975: as a teacher, encouragement had become his motto,

'. . . dating back to the time when my dreamy indolence at secondary school was jolted by a teacher who saw in my exercise book the words, "the grand horror of the uplifted sea", and exclaimed: "Boy, you're a poet!"

'That was my "Pauline" conversion, my road to Damascus,' he recalled. 'I had to be good at something and in the next seven years I memorised 5,000 lines of poetry.'

A later article by Tony Moxon, another BGS master, noted:

. . . training was by apprenticeship – he became 'Pupil-Teacher Stanley'! In those days, before 1914, the size of class could depend on the ability of the teacher. Even as a trainee, giving demonstrations of elementary science, he taught a class of 120. Classes of 50 were common. Yet he has known teachers who were incapable of controlling 10.

By the time of his death in 1985, aged 97, SCG had amassed an assortment of Bachelor and Masters degrees in English, French, Latin and latterly, during the years of his retirement, Italian, conferred by the universities of Birmingham, London and Liverpool. Needless to say, his descendants are still waiting for evidence of this gene to reappear.

Back to the early 1920s and he was recognised as a scholar of note holding a variety of posts including lecturer at Oxford University and reader, adviser and critic to publishers, notably the Oxford Press. He was also busy in Bradford establishing the first English Department in the history of the school and teaching, among others, the young Denis Healey, now Baron Healey of Riddlesden, and the eminent historian Alan Bullock. In 1981 a school magazine article by Tony Moxon commented:

There was then no English department, and for several years he was the only English teacher. It had previously been considered that English could be picked up as a by-product of Classics, and Glassey had to fight hard to establish the independence of his subject.

Teacher Stanley . . .

By the 1930s he had become something of an authority on the teaching of English grammar and had a string of 17 textbooks to his credit.

The 'Groundwork' series became known affectionately (or otherwise) to countless numbers of pupils across Britain and her colonies, as their 'glass-eyes'. Published by Oxford University Press, they were written between 1934–47 and focused on grammar (covered in two parts), poetry, composition, précis and criticism. They were re-printed many times and he was still receiving royalty payments in the 1970s. As a footnote, it was SCG who is credited with having introduced comprehension testing as a means of teaching the rudiments of English grammar to generations of pupils. This was one achievement which was grossly under-rated by his ungrateful and unscholarly grandchildren.

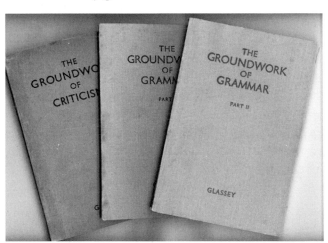

Mum recalled how the family had had to keep very quiet in the house during the long summer holidays so they did not disturb the author, both when at school and later on during the war when she was working as a doctor and living at home. My own earliest memories of Grandpa are of him sitting at the desk in his study with his green eye shade on, and feeling the heat from the angle-poise lamp shining close to his work due to his failing eyesight. We children were expected to be quiet too and that wasn't easy when there were four of us and a dog!

SCG was a cigarette smoker in his early days, but for as long as anyone could remember he took snuff. Tony Moxon again:

For Old Boys of the 1920s, 30s and 40s, the name Stanley Glassey will recall a domed forehead, a resonant and rich voice, the curiosity of seeing snuff taken . . .

'Underdown', in Otford, Kent.

We children revelled in the ritual: silver snuff box out of jacket pocket, lid flicked open; small, mother of pearl penknife out of trouser pocket, blade exposed; measured quantity of evil-smelling, orange-coloured powder expertly conveyed to heel of left thumb and then, tilting elbow ever so slightly, lifted to a waiting flared nostril, sharp sniff, and then repeated again for the other nostril. Residue down front of cardigan. Nobody else did this: it was wonderful to watch and evidence of his habit can clearly be seen in nearly every photograph taken of him. Never since have I seen anyone take snuff; and this tobacco-smoking, snuff-inhaling, gentleman broke all the rules and very nearly made it to his century.

My grandparents retired to live in Kent in 1949 and during my early childhood in the 1950s we stayed with them at 'Underdown', their lovely bungalow in Hillydeal Road, nestling under Greenhill Wood in the then idyllic Kent village of Otford.

'Gangan'.

Gangan was a creative, resourceful woman, a keen bridge player and wonderful grandmother to us and our cousins. She took care of all the practicalities – driving, maintenance in both house and garden, everything – just as she had always done, leaving Stanley to read, write and think.

They both loved their garden which gently sloped uphill to the fringe of the woods which you could get to through a rickety wooden gate set in the boundary fence. He grew tomatoes, apples, peaches and nectarines (and more books). They took holidays in his beloved Italy and on one memorable occasion while swinging between peaks in a cable car, my rather befuddled grandpa horrified fellow travellers when he got up out of his seat and made to leave by the door. Only fast work on behalf of Gangan saved him from a premature demise. All this was then relayed by postcard to the families back home!

Memories flood back: the smell inside the revolving summer house (which is still there in the back garden); daffodils everywhere, for we always stayed a week at Easter; 'Duckingham Palace', the little house in the centre of the village pond built for the ducks; watching their tame blackbird 'Sweetie', who each morning would hop into the kitchen and take titbits off a dish; and being soundly chastised for disappearing one morning without a word, to help the milkman on his horse and cart make deliveries down the lane. Well, I was only 5 and for a while they must have been worried sick.

The idyll came to a sad and abrupt end when the following year, 1960, our lovely Gangan died early one October evening just as they were settling down to watch a programme on the television. Grandpa was bereft. My mother and uncle Bill packed up his house and he came to live with us in Wirral as we had a spare room. No-one, least of all my mother, gave him more than six months but as time went on he immersed himself

Young Elizabeth and brother Billy.

in his academic work, his book-lined bed-sitting room doubling as his study. His day started at seven; he would venture downstairs at mealtimes and go for his daily two-mile walk before lunch. After a post-prandial nap he resumed his studies, pausing only for afternoon tea and then supper until it was time for his late night whisky and then bed. And spelling lessons on a Friday afternoon soon became a regular part of our lives.

He took holidays at the same time each year; two weeks, twice a year with his son and the family in Beverley in east Yorkshire and six weeks of cricket in the summer staying in hotels in Edgbaston and Canterbury. In the early 1960s, having commenced Italian at Liverpool University, he resumed his travels to Italy, attending summer schools at the universities of Florence and Perugia. However, with the advent of the Labour government's £50 limit (on taking currency out of the country) sadly these trips were curtailed never to be taken again.

Returning to my mother's childhood, in 1923 Joan started school at the age of five and on being asked what she was called, decided to use her middle name replying, 'Elizabeth.' It wasn't until she had to learn to write it that she reflected that perhaps Joan would have been much easier. So outside the family 'Elizabeth' was how she was known.

Throughout her childhood the family lived at 77 Athol Road, in the Heaton area of Bradford (with hindsight this would prove to be quite a coincidence!). She was good-natured and grew up happy and secure. One of her earliest memories was the regular Sunday afternoon visit to the Cartwright Hall Art Gallery in Lister Park. This outing became something of a ritual, with father and mother accompanied by Joan and Billy. When she was about five years old, Joan was asked one Saturday if she wanted to go to 'the pictures' with Billy and his friends; she quickly declined the offer and continued to do so over the next couple of years, fondly believing that he was going to the Art Gallery. She was nearly seven before she realised that he was in fact going to the Picture House to see the moving pictures. How cheated she felt at the lost opportunity.

At the age of 11 she gained a place at Bradford Grammar School for Girls where she was a good all-rounder. At the end of her first year at the school she was introduced to Patricia Franklyn. Pat, as she was known, was the elder daughter of Dr and Mrs Franklyn, her father being a well-respected radiologist in the city. It was during a consultation with Dr Franklyn that Elizabeth's mother heard that his 11-year-old daughter was returning from boarding school in Dolgellau, North Wales to take up a place at the grammar school too. Lilian offered to introduce the two girls during the holidays and Pat and Elizabeth quickly became firm friends, sharing so many things including holidays in Anglesey, the Isle of Wight and Norfolk; it was a friendship that was destined to last a lifetime.

Elizabeth (left) and Pat on holiday in Shanklin, Isle of Wight 1936.

During the holiday at Shanklin, on 30 August 1936, the two girls stood at the top of the beach and watched as the cruise liner, SS *Queen Mary*, raced past the shore heading for Southampton. It was making its historic bid to win the coveted Blue Riband Award for the fastest crossing of the Atlantic by an ocean liner – and it succeeded. (The Cunard White Star liner made the voyage in three days, 23 hours and 57 minutes, averaging 30.63 knots. She was to win the record once more on 14 August 1938 shaving three hours 15 minutes off her previous best).

Elizabeth and Pat wouldn't forget the spectacle, nor that of watching the excited crowds lower down the beach get inundated as the wake from the *Queen Mary* hit the shore!

Nine years later the same ship would pass the same beach bringing her fiancé back to Britain after almost five years away.

It was while on holiday with the Franklyns at Benllech Bay in Angelsey that Dr Cunningham from Wirral (another coincidence which would later become apparent), another of the Franklyn circle who was staying with them, noticed that Elizabeth had a goitre (enlarged thyroid gland), heralding the beginnings of the thyroid problems that would affect her throughout her adult life. Then at the age of 17, she developed septicaemia which was complicated by streptococcal pneumonia and very nearly proved to be fatal. Let down by an inept and pompous family doctor, only swift intervention and a change of medical opinion saved the day. The new physician decided to try an experimental M & B (May and Baker) product called Prontosil, a forerunner of today's antibiotics and she was one of the first patients to be treated with it in Bradford; thankfully it worked. Elizabeth rallied and though significantly weakened by the illness she recovered. She had an uphill battle to complete and pass her final year at school. However, she was determined to follow in Bill's shoes (he was by now a medical student in Leeds) and after an extra year at school her hard work paid off with good results. This was also Pat's chosen career and a year earlier, in October 1936, she had gone up to the medical school in St Andrews on the east coast of Scotland. She had suffered from recurrent chest ailments and it was felt that the bracing north-easterly climate would be far healthier for her.

It must have been a worrying time for Elizabeth's parents; they knew what a financial strain it would be to put their daughter through medical school too. But, thanks to Dr Franklyn's advice they found a way. He had been a tremendous support to Stanley and Lilian when Elizabeth was so ill, advising on the change of medical opinion at that critical time. Once again he recommended the course of treatment they should follow: Elizabeth, like Pat, must go away to university in the interest of her health and where better than St Andrews. So she was packed off on the train in the autumn of 1937.

The first Saturday night 'hop' of the year was cause, I expect, for much preparation and excitement at 'Kinnessburn'. Elizabeth (or Liz, as she became known to her friends) and her room-mate Isobel (Bunty) Fernback were joined by Pat and some of the other 2nd years, all going along together. Held at the Men's Union in North Street, the band would have been playing the favourite warm-up number of the era, Glenn Miller's classic 'In the Mood' when they arrived, as they did each week to get things going. Popular tunes such as 'Smoke Gets in Your Eyes', 'Anything Goes' and 'The Way You Look Tonight' were other favourites that got a regular airing.

Liz met a 2nd year student called Atholl Duncan and Bunty met fellow medical student, John Forfar. Atholl said that it was her striking blue eyes that first caught his attention. They would to hold it for the next 60 years. The two pairs would remain as couples and friends, eventually getting married when the war was over. To their friends, Atholl and Elizabeth became known as the 'twin souls'.

Thankfully they and the other young couples did at least have some peace time left in which to enjoy getting to know each other before the curtain fell. The memories of these days would help sustain many of them when, all too soon, they were separated for who knew how long.

As a person Liz was a 'giver'. Witty and intelligent with a well-developed sense of fun, she was also naturally modest, a discreet and attentive listener who had a way of quietly instilling confidence in others. This sensitive young woman was destined for a profession where a healthy sense of humour was required in almost equal measure to academic and practical skills. It would help her cope with such a demanding and stressful job and to survive not only the immediate future but for the rest of her life when she would have to face so many hurdles.

Elizabeth (4th row from front, 6th from left) and students of University Hall 1938.

Chapter 3

War Begins

1939–1940

In September 1939 Atholl, along with thousands of others, put his life on hold and joined His Majesty's Forces to fight in another war. Those three years spent training with the university's OTC now stood him in good stead. He had enjoyed the camaraderie of the male-dominated military world, he was fit and like so many of his generation he had a deep sense of duty which he faced, by and large, with a healthy sense of humour.

He wanted to join the RAF but eye problems precluded his acceptance for pilot training and he wouldn't consider compromise by accepting ground crew work. They recommended that he came back to them in six months' time but Atholl was impatient and instead he took a commission in the Highland Light Infantry (HLI) as a 2nd Lieutenant.

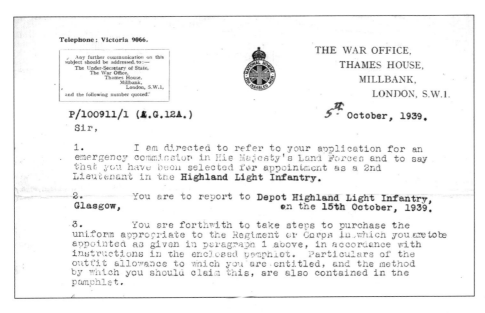

Notice of sign-up.

Training commenced in early October at Maryhill Barracks in Glasgow (like the Regiment now long gone, buried under new housing developments). It quickly dawned on him that infantry troops walk everywhere; not good news for someone who had inherited bunions on both feet! During

Vickers Machine Gun course, Palace Barrack, Hollywood, Belfast, 1939. Atholl is fifth from left front row, lying propped up on his elbow.

the summer of that year he had volunteered for a Vickers machine gun training camp in Northern Ireland (see above) and he decided that now was the time to put this experience to good use and so put in for a transfer to the Argyll and Sutherland Highlanders (A&SH) machine gun unit.

Events overtook him and in early January 1940, attached to No. 3 Company HLI, 2nd Lieutenant Duncan arrived in France as part of the BEF (British Expeditionary Force). Once there he quickly gained promotion to Lieutenant and his transfer to the Argylls came through. Happily for his feet, machine gun detachments rode everywhere on the back of trucks.

Initially he was stationed at Le Mans before being drafted to the front at Arras in late January. Within a week he had been admitted to the military hospital in Dieppe where he spent three weeks being treated for pneumonia, after which he was posted back again to Le Mans. In the first week of May 1940, back home in St Andrews for seven days' leave, he and Elizabeth became engaged and, after she had spoken to her parents on the telephone, Atholl sent them a letter formally setting out his intentions for the future.

In keeping with the resourcefulness imposed by wartime conditions, the engagement ring, a diamond surrounded by pearls, was fashioned from what had previously been one of his mother's stick pins. The happy couple, together with his parents and sister Bunty, then took a rare day off and headed to the Highlands to celebrate.

His return to France was short-lived and soon hundreds of thousands of Allied troops were being picked up off the beaches at Dunkirk in a desperate fight for survival. Further west on the Cotenin Peninsula, a week or so later he and his men were being evacuated through Cherbourg docks to Southampton.

Atholl's letter to
Elizabeth's parents.

Mansefield,
St. Andrews
Fife
5·5·40.

Dear Mr & Mrs Glassey,

I was so pleased to get your telephone message on Friday night; I intended to write you then to ask your consent and I am very pleased you approve of our engagement. Of course we do not contemplate marriage for a few years yet as Elizabeth wishes to complete her studies and I do not think it would be fair to either of us if we were married whilst I am on active service.

I, too, intend to complete my studies when I am demobilised after the war and to apply myself so that I will be able to offer Elizabeth a comfortable home

Hoping you are all enjoying the best of health and adding all kind wishes

Yours very sincerely

Atholl.

Elizabeth at the time of
her engagement.

On leave from BEF, May 1940 – a trip to the Highlands to celebrate the engagement – left to right: Bunty, Elizabeth, Atholl's mother, Atholl.

Once there, he had the distinction of being one of the few members of the Argylls 5th Battalion which were then promptly sent back to France to cover the final retreat, as part of a hurriedly convened second expeditionary force under General Brooke. They were evacuated for the second and final time (once again from Cherbourg) in mid-June of that year.

Back in the United Kingdom an intensive programme of re-training commenced and he spent the next six months travelling the length of the British Isles, from Cornwall to Seaton Carew in the north east, from Glasgow to Askrigg in the Yorkshire Dales.

The young couple did manage to snatch a few days here and there between his postings and Elizabeth's intensive workload. Now that she was doing clinical training she was spending much of her time travelling to and from Dundee by train for lectures and hospital placements. Though the distance was not great these journeys could be tedious as the train would often be delayed on the Fife side of the Tay Bridge if there was an air raid warning in Dundee. Despite so frequently being unavoidably delayed, no quarter was given by irate and cantankerous professors (many of whom had come out of retirement to ease staff shortages) and who regularly berated

Leaving Cherbourg docks for the second and last time, June 1940. Taken by 2nd Lieutenant Duncan.

their unlucky students.

On the rare occasions when time and petrol rationing allowed, Atholl would take his fiancée, parents and sister Bunty for a run up to the Highlands. They visited the places where the family had spent holidays in the caravan when he was a child. Such vivid recollections would prove invaluable to him during the years of isolation that were ahead. For now though, these day trips provided such a welcome break for them all.

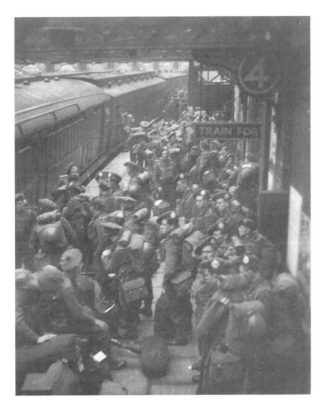

West Hartlepool station platform – October 1940 (taken by 2nd Lieutenant Duncan).

No. 8 Platoon, 6th Battalion A&SH, North Yorkshire Moors, October 1940 – 2nd Lieutenant Duncan took this photo of 'his Jocks'.

Chapter 4

Peace and War

Jan 1941–March 1942

His orders and travel warrant arrived on 4 January 1941. There were just 24 hours left of his leave before 2nd Lieutenant Duncan had to report to Stirling Castle. His father then drove him the fifty miles or so and said farewell.

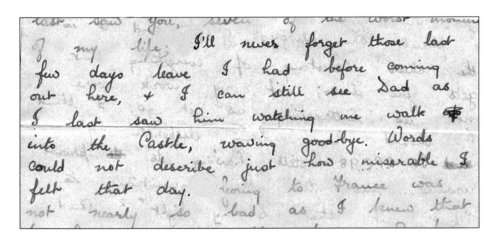

Within a few days he had sailed from Glasgow for the Far East, destination Singapore. The troop ship they were on headed up the Clyde and out into the Atlantic, initially in a north-westerly direction to avoid U-boat activity. Once in safer waters they headed south but had to make port at least once along the coast of West Africa to avoid the enemy.

While initially his letters were positive, very soon the novelty of life at sea wore off. He could only describe the humdrum existence on board the crowded ship as censorship rules meant he was unable to disclose where they were and what he'd seen.

Rounding the Cape of Good Hope the ship anchored in Cape Town for two days for re-fuelling and taking on more provisions, before sailing up the eastern seaboard of Africa to Mombasa. While lying at anchor there he bumped into a fellow St Andrews undergraduate on deck one morning. The final leg of the journey took them across the Indian Ocean to Bombay and then on to their final destination. The beauty of the last part of the voyage remained with him for the rest of his life.

2/Lt. AaDuncan
A + S.H.
(RACA)
~~STIRLING CASTLE~~ c/o A.P.O. 750
~~SCOTLAND~~   6·1·41

TELEPHONE
STIRLING. 260.

My darling Elizabeth,
                    Just a
short note to let you know
that I am still in the
land of the living and am
having an exceedingly fine
time on board ship; the
boat itself is very luxurious
considering it is a troop ship
and our quarters are very
comfortable.
You will note that my
address has been changed
so will you be so good
as to check it with the
one I gave the folks as I
think I missed out the serial

TELEPHONE
STIRLING. 260.

STIRLING CASTLE
SCOTLAND

letters "R.A.C.A." when I gave
it to them.
As most of the news I could
give you would most
certainly be censored I shall
close now so wishing you
the best of luck,
        all love from
            Atholl. xxxxx

His first letter from the troop ship en route to Singapore.

During this time, Atholl kept up his correspondence with Elizabeth and the family, both of whom he was missing terribly. His letters and telegrams reached home and were treasured and in them were frequent references to his new nephew George, Nesta's first child, who was just over two months old when Atholl had left Scotland. He resented missing out on being an uncle for the first time.

His need to correspond, initially by letter and later with his diary, underpins the story of his struggle to survive. He needed to keep the family and his beloved Elizabeth close by him; after all, apart from his brief adventure in France he had not been away from home for any length of time. They would help him to get through whatever was to come, however long it took to do the job and return home again. However, within the limits imposed by the censors, his letters during the coming months painted vivid pictures of what life was like across on the other side of the world.

He was just 23 years old when they finally steamed into Keppel Harbour in early March 1941. Mercifully, the voyage had been pretty uneventful

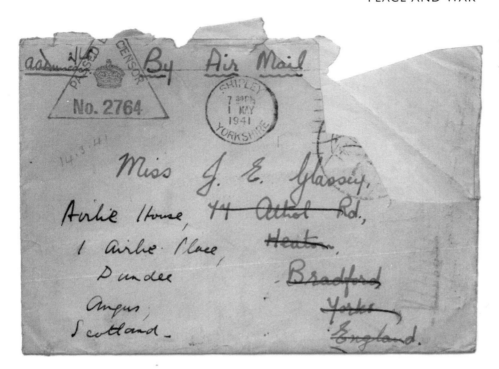

Note the censor's mark on the envelope. He later removed the stamp for his collection.

Telegram dated 12 March 1941, notified the family of his safe arrival in Singapore.

unlike many of the convoys that were to make the same journey over the next few months. Singapore seemed like a haven of peace after war-torn Britain.

Once ashore 2nd Lieutenant Duncan immediately found himself involved in an intensive programme of jungle warfare training in Kranji marshes, in preparation for the likelihood of hand-to-hand combat. The

2nd Lieutenant Duncan in
tropical kit at Tyersall Park.

The Officers' Mess, Tyersall Park, Singapore,
1941, taken by 2nd Lieutenant Duncan.

The photo of a monkey
that he took in the jungle.

troops had to endure many discomforts, wading through swamps and across rivers with leeches and snakes, not to mention disease, among the hazards they had to negotiate. Among his collection of photographs there is just one photograph he took in the jungle (see left).

In early 2001, when I was reading through the correspondence written at this time, I found a reference to a newsreel film crew and a photographer from *LIFE* magazine which were documenting one of these training exercises (see bottom, opposite).

Thanks to the wonders of the world wide web I found the edition of *LIFE* magazine which features the photographs taken on that day. It was published on 21 July 1941.

I sent off for an original copy and when it arrived I was fascinated to see that it had on the back cover a printed address block naming the original owner (presumably a subscriber to *LIFE*). The magazine contained a six-page spread on Singapore, documenting the economy, political and social scene and, most

Painting pictures with words . . .

No. 6.

2nd Batt. A.+ S.H.
Malaya
21. 3. 41.

Dear All,
        Just a few lines to let you know that I am still "in the pink" and have settled down to life out here, although I find the heat pretty ghastly at times. A few nights ago, I was out on a scheme in the jungle (my first) and found it very interesting: now, before I arrived here my ideas of jungle had been formed from the shots of it I had seen in pictures, but the real article is vastly different, being so dense in parts that a person could be standing ten yards in front of you + would be completely out of sight. Snakes, including King Cobras 10' long, centipedes 10" long, scorpions, elephants, tigers, monkeys, tarantulas, ants, mosquitoes, + a host of other "beasties" all tend to lend colour + interest to the place. Most animals depart at high speed – including the snakes – on the approach of humans but it is rather eerie at night when halted to hear all the sounds of the jungle.

Mention of the *LIFE* photographer in a letter dated 7 April 1941.

The other day, we did a swamp + river crossing for the benefit of some news-reel camera men + a photographer from the American magazine "Life" so if you watch the newsreel bills at home you may see your one + only boy floundering about in water + mud, as they definitely took a few pictures of my platoon. What we called them at the time is nobodys business.!!!!

Members of the famous
Highland regiment
(A & SH) crossing a
swamp during exercises.
(By kind permission of
The Straits Times,
Singpaore.)

Air Chief Marshal Sir
Robert Brooke-Popham
heading a conference at
Singapore Naval base
HQ.
(By kind permission of
The Straits Times, Singa-
pore.)

importantly at that time, the military build-up under way to defend the
fortress island.

To underline the significance of the preparations being made in the
British colony, and perhaps as a consequence of Churchill's tactics to
engage the sympathy of the American people and win over their support
for Britain, the readership of *LIFE* was, that week, greeted with a front
cover of the magazine, dominated by a portrait of the British Commander-
in-Chief in Singapore, Air Chief Marshal Sir Robert Brooke-Popham. The
whole magazine makes very interesting reading in view of the fact that
America was not yet at war and the editorial gives an insight into the prevailing view at the time.

In a letter to the family in the summer of 1941, Atholl writes about his
meeting and conversations with 'Brookham' as he was affectionately known.

Chatham Court:
his new digs, much
better than the barracks.

A couple of months after his arrival in Singapore, while in the town one day, he bumped into Mac (Captain Angus Maclean) a friend whom he had not seen around for a while. Atholl enquired what he'd been up to and was intrigued to learn that Mac had been re-assigned to Intelligence Corps work which he was enjoying immensely. He was delighted when Mac suggested that he should join him as they urgently needed cipher officers and it should be right up his street. So, seeing his opportunity to escape the discomforts and hazards of the swamps and jungle training, and with Mac saying he would see to the transfer details, Atholl readily agreed. Back

Telegram to his parents
informing them of his
new job.

at the office, despite the protestations of his immediate superiors, 2nd Lieutenant Duncan's transfer was rubber-stamped and he was released forthwith.

I make reference here to the regimental history of the period which offers a fascinating glimpse of military thinking on the ground at the time. Written by Brigadier Stewart, *The History of the Argyll & Sutherland Highlanders 2nd Battalion 1939–45* includes an authoritative account of the lead up to the Malayan Campaign of 1941–42, which culminated in the biggest single disaster in British military history, the surrender of the garrison of Singapore. In chapter 1 at the top of page 6 he writes:

'. . . The Battalion was continually milked of its best for other jobs; drafts arrived from U.K. . . . and were then picked over . . . by staff and services vultures . . .'

This perhaps goes some way to explaining the objections made by his superiors when they learned of 2nd Lieutenant Duncan's impending move. He was being poached.

Promoted to Lieutenant he got his pips (although it would not be gazetted – appear in the *London Gazette* – for another five months). One thing that delighted him at about this time, was that he was present in Singapore for a moment in philatelic history. On May 6 he wrote home telling them that his letter was to be sent on what he described as the trans-Pacific and trans-Atlantic air mail service. This was the inaugural flight of the 'Clipper Service' – the Pan-American Airways' service from San Francisco to Malaya – which would take-off on 9 May. He asked them to let him know in their next letter how long it had taken to arrive and that if there was a great saving in time, he would use the service again. Although their reply did not survive, it must have proved effective because the envelopes kept from his subsequent letters to Elizabeth were addressed:

Letter sent to Elizabeth on the inaugural flight of the 'Clipper Service'. Note the censor's mark.

and his letter of 3 June to his folks, opened with the following remark,

> Chattam Court
> 2, St. Thomas Walk
> Singapore
> 3.6.41
>
> Dear All,
> The trans-Pacific Clipper has just soared overhead, outward bound for America and so I know it is time to sit down and start another letter as it generally takes me about ten days to compose one.

He moved residence a couple of times and began to enjoy life more. His letters and a series of photographs taken at the time tell their own story.

A friend of mine out here has just bought a cine-camera and has been taking various local scenes with it so that when he returns home, he can show his folks just what this place is like. He then told me that when he was showing that film he would close all the windows, turn the central heating full on, build up a huge fire and dry a lot of damp towels before it to give them an idea of the atmosphere. When the views of Singapore river were being shown, a few rotten eggs smashed would give a close approximation to the smell, whilst the evening scenes would be shown to the accompaniment of Chinese music – a lot of cymbal beating, and interspersed with peculiar wails and 'plink-plonk sounds – played on the gramophone, while he rushed about jabbing needles into the audience to represent the mosquitoes. This may seem rather far-fetched to you but it is really quite an accurate description of life out here.

I myself have taken a good few snaps since I arrived and am putting them all in an album so that you will be able to see, for yourself, some typical scenes from the East . . . [Sadly this album did not survive.]

. . . Often, in the evenings, I sit outside and picture all the places I want to be, people I want to see, and things I want to do, but am always brought back to earth by either the mosquitoes or the smell of Chinese cooking, which defies description . . .

Lieutenant Duncan (left) with Colonel Pearson choosing fabrics for the ladies back home: 'No. 1 piecework' is the caption on the back.

Atholl's Private Pilot's Certificate and Licence (Flying Machines).

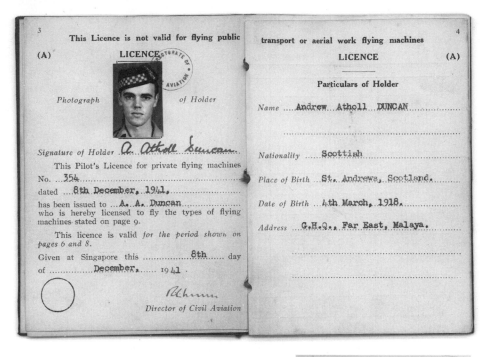

Left:
The badge of the Royal Singapore Flying Club, now known as Republic of Singapore Flying Club.

Right:
Lieutenant Duncan standing beside the trainer he had just landed.

During the early summer months he used what little spare time he had to realise a lifetime ambition and set about getting his private pilot's licence. He joined the Royal Singapore Flying Club and spent every spare moment taking lessons eventually gaining his licence and certificate in early December 1941, just in the nick of time.

During August he wrote home telling them of Japan's increasingly threatening actions but reassuring the folks at home.

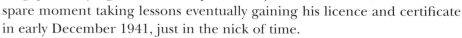

. . . The papers and the wireless are all giving great prominence to Japan's latest move and the democracies prompt reply, and while, to you at home, it may seem a very sudden and grave step, we out here know that Japan might do that and consequently have been little perturbed by it. I can assure you of one point, if they try any monkey business with us, they will get smacked so hard that they won't know what has hit them . . .

His letters to Elizabeth tried to express his feelings for her, his pride at her success in the exams as well as requests to her to write and tell him what sort of things he should buy for her and the family, as so many items were available out there that were just a distant memory back in Britain.

My Darling Elizabeth,

Your letter, giving the news of your success in the degree exams has just arrived, and I am so pleased and proud of you; I am quite sure that next year at this time I shall be addressing my letters to you as Dr Glassey. . . . I am enclosing a copy of a snapshot which I took of myself and hope you like it . . . I am afraid that there has been a long interval since my last letter but for once I am not to blame, the reason being that the "Clipper" has been held up for a fortnight now at the Phillipines and is arriving here two weeks overdue. However, prior to this delay my letters should have been arriving about once a fortnight as I have not missed a single Clipper despatch since the service was inaugurated in April.

Summer will be over now in Britain and Christmas is getting near which means cold weather and long nights for you back home, but for us out here, there are no seasons and likely as not we will spend Xmas Day sweating as much as usual, longing to be back with you all again. I think that I shall be tempted to roll naked in the first snow I see, for a cool day out here is quite unknown; even the water in the bathing pool and the sea is tepid and it is no good thinking a swim will cool you down as the very effort of swimming makes you sweat like a pig as soon as you get out of the water . . .

Letter written on 9 September 1941 detailing the discomforts of life in the Tropics.

Below:
The photograph which he mentioned in letter (top left) written on 17 October 1941.

He numbered all her letters as they arrived and was able to say in early autumn that he had received all but No. 7 which,

'. . . I am afraid is now lying somewhere at the bottom of the Atlantic as No. 10 was the latest one I have received . . .'

Memories of home were vivid and at times they combined with feelings of shame that he was somehow 'having it easy'.

. . . At times, I feel almost a shirker, being out here, where the war seems so very distant, living, comparatively speaking, in the lap of luxury, with no blackout, bombs etc. However, it was none of my doing that brought me out here, and, Heaven only knows, I would much rather be back home . . .

Posted to the family back home, this large annual was full of interesting articles and full colour advertisements.
(By kind permission of *The Straits Times*, Singapore.)

Pictured on p. 25 of *The Straits Times Annual*: the California Clipper landing at Singapore to inaugurate the Pan-American Airways service from San Francisco to Malaya.
(By kind permission of *The Straits Times*, Singapore.)

To help them to visualise something of the life he was now engaged in, he sent home a copy of the *Straits Times Annual*, a pictorial magazine depicting life in the colony, published by Singapore's leading newspaper. He also posted one off to Alec Rattray, a family friend living in California.

The articles were interspersed with numerous advertisements for products made famous by Imperial economic development, many of which are still household names: Kelvinator refrigerators, Chivers preserves and tinned goods, proclaiming themselves "the finest English products you can buy" and Innoxa beauty preparations, to name just three. The articles were illustrated with scores of black and white photographs depicting the recent military developments, and featured news about the different sections of the Allied Forces which arrived throughout the year: British, Australian Imperial Forces (AIF), the Indian regiments and Malay Forces. A seven-page article under the heading 'The Dollar Arsenal and a Mighty Fortress', featured a photograph captioned 'members of the famous Highland regiment crossing a swamp during exercises', evidence of yet another photocall for the Argylls. It also featured photographs of the 'California Clipper' arriving at Singapore and lying at the flying boat anchorage in the harbour, emblazoned with both the 'Stars and Stripes' and the 'Union Jack'.

In a letter written on 12 November 1941 he tried to allay fears for his safety at this time, which from the family's viewpoint had been compounded by him choosing to engage in such a dangerous pursuit as flying.

> *. . . I get very little flying these days as we are having the rainy season just now and consequently the weather conditions are anything but ideal for flying. I think I can hear you heaving a very large sigh of relief and wishing that we had a rainy season all the year round but again I should like to emphasise that there is no danger at all so you need not worry . . .*

He sent presents home for birthdays and Christmas and fretted about their safe arrival as so much shipping was being attacked and sunk. For her birthday that year Elizabeth received from him a handbag made from crocodile skin which she treasured. He, too, received a very special Christmas present from her, an embroidery she had done of the regimental badge of the Argyll and Sutherland Highlanders. It is the only piece of embroidery I know of that my mother did, a true labour of love, though goodness only knows when she found the time to do it. He immediately had it framed. She had used as her guide, a painting of the badge that Atholl had previously done on a 9-inch square, three-quarter-inch thick piece of oak. Amazingly, this precious piece of needlework not only survived the journey out to him but also his sojourn over the next four years. To this day it still hangs in the

family home and is a tangible reminder of the hope for the future that they both shared at that time.

In late November Lieutenant Duncan was invited to a cocktail party to celebrate the 1st anniversary of the GHQFE (General Headquarters Far East). Following this Brooke-Popham invited him to another less formal occasion.

> . . . A few days later I got an invitation from him to go and have dinner and then go to a flick-show afterwards and was more than pleased with this latter invitation, for, after all, he is the C-in-C, and I am only a very junior Lieutenant, and many officers, far senior to me, would do anything to receive such an invitation. However, once I got there I felt quite at ease for 'Brookham' chatted about this, that and everything and asked questions about St A. etc. . . .

Above:
Elizabeth's embroidery of the Regimental badge. This was a Christmas present to Atholl. He received it in November 1941.

As November drew to a close and the tensions increased, his need to keep his family close to him was undiminished. As the situation deteriorated he was frantically busy and it was not until 6 December that he found time to write to both the family and Elizabeth, adding to both letters over the next few days. To Elizabeth he refers to the needlework telling her,

> I have had the beautiful crest you embroidered for me framed and it now reposes on my dressing table in the honoured position between your two photographs and has been much admired . . . The political situation out here at the present is far from being reassuring and by the time that this reaches you, I expect that the issue of peace or war in the Far East will have been decided, one way or the other, but speaking for myself, I do not care which way it is, as Japan will have to see reason before any lasting peace can be ensured and, if she chooses to do things the hard way, à la Hitler, I am more than confident that our navy, army and air force can adequately administer the necessary thrashing which she so richly deserves.

He finishes both this letter and the one to his parents with a PS, written on 13 December, in which he acknowledges the news that Britain was now at war with Japan and tries his best to reassure them. To allay their immediate worries he had also sent a cable the previous day:

Telegram from Lieutenant Duncan to his family sent on 12 December 1941.

It must have been a frightening time and he drew strength and hope from their letters. Although there are many instances when he must have felt desperately low he never gave up the hope that he would eventually return home.

By late January 1942, the writing was on the wall. The defending forces were being pressed by the Japanese who were advancing down the Malayan peninsula.

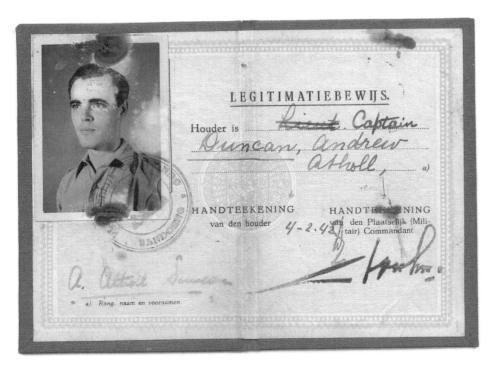

Lieutenant Duncan's Dutch East Indies military pass issued on arrival in Java. This has been altered to Captain after his promotion.

At the same time, British GHQ was making preparations to transfer to Lembang, near the town of Bandoeng in Java. Of the four cipher officers attached to GHQ, two were married and two were single; when they were told that two could be evacuated from Singapore to the relative safety of India, Lieutenant Des Campion and Captain Duncan decided they should volunteer to stay on, allowing the two who were married to get away. Once GHQ was established on Java it came under the direct control of the Dutch High Command based on the island.

Telegram from Lieutenant Duncan to the family dated 3 February 1942.

Reply from, first of all, Atholl's father on 7 February 1942 . . .

In early February he sent the following messages home from his new base at GHQ in the mountains of central Java, informing them among other things that he had been promoted to captain, with a reply from his father on 7 February and then his mother on 19 February.

Dated 16 February 1942, the day after the fall of Singapore, telling his family of his promotion.

...followed by one from his mother, 19 February 1942.

The only letter from home which has survived from this period (written in February 1942) is one that he never received; written by Elizabeth on 12 February 1942 (see Chapter 8, page 133) it was returned home to her later that spring, undelivered. In early June, just before her finals, another bundle of letters were returned to her which nearly broke her heart (these letters have not survived).

None of the mail that he received while in Singapore survived as it had to be destroyed once they were on the run and the Japs were closing in. The following extract from his narrative explains what happened:

> *That night at dinner, Col. Russell told us that the entire HQ would be leaving (Lembang) for a secret destination in the early hours of the following morning and to get packed and be ready to move at a moment's notice. Unfortunately both Des and myself had a fair amount of kit at the dhobie, so once again our wardrobe diminished in size. A final sort out of kit and destruction of personal papers occupied the next hour or two . . .*

His final communiqué to his family was on his 24th birthday, 4 March 1942.

His last telegram – still trying to reassure the family.

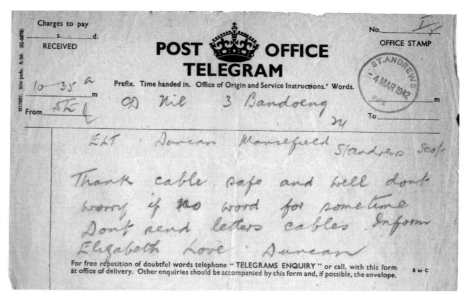

He had to wait two long years, until 9 March 1944, before he would receive his next letter. Although many would be sent, few survived, some of them being returned to Britain unopened marked 'return to sender'. The first letter he received in captivity was from Elizabeth and had been written on 15 July 1943. He marked it 'No. 1' and added the date he received it, a process he repeated with every new letter or card. By that time he had moved to his third camp, Zentsuji, an officers' camp on the island of Shikoku, one of the four main islands which make up Japan.

Four days after he sent the cable on his birthday, he started to keep a diary and its first entries are reproduced on page 1.

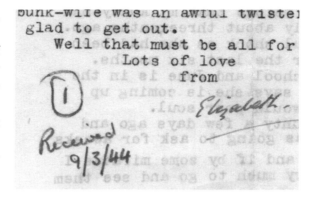

Atholl marked every piece of mail he received with the date and a number.

His arrival at the prison camp at Tandjong Priok on 27 March, was heralded by him collapsing on the station platform suffering from malaria.

By the end of that month, he had no idea of how long it would be before he could once again hold Elizabeth's hand, walk down Market Street or play a round of golf on the Old Course.

Tandjong Priok station – a pre-war postcard.

Chapter 5

Java, Jeopardy and Jail: The Start of Their Captivity

Batavia.
Chineesche woningen.

Chinese village settlements close to the camp – left and opposite, pre-war postcards.

March–October 1942

Tandjong Priok was, and still is, the dock area to the east of Batavia (now known as Jakarta), the capital of Java. It was several miles from the centre of the city and the area was a renowned fever spot. Now it became home to a large POW transit camp (or Uniekampong) which is where my father found himself, suffering from malaria, on 29 March 1942. During the summer of 1942 approximately 4,500 prisoners were held at the camp.

Another British soldier among the first party to arrive in the camp, was a young man named John Baxter, a plumber by trade who was serving as a craftsman with the Royal Engineers. He and other British engineers had been sent to Tandjong Priok a week or so prior to the arrival of the bulk of the new inmates. The Japanese set the men to work fencing off the compound, which was roughly a mile square, with barbed wire ready for the impending arrival of large numbers of prisoners of war. In addition to the perimeter fencing, individual compounds within the camp were also separately wired off. Having been left more or less to their own devices, they set about this task with efficiency and a determination not to do too good a job of it. They left several points around the perimeter not properly secured, as an insurance policy to be redeemed before too long. During the following months these openings proved to be very useful, allowing regular forays to be made to the outlying Chinese and native settlements. Once this job was completed, and new arrivals had settled in, the engineers pressed the Japanese to allow them to tackle the urgent task of organising an adequate water supply and drainage system for the camp.

This information I gleaned thanks to reading John Baxter's book *Not Much of a Picnic*. He self-published his book in 1995 and having got hold of a copy, I was delighted to find out that I could get in touch with him. Since then, we have corresponded regularly and he has filled in a great deal of detail about the setting up of Tandjong Priok. The following is quoted from his letter dated 4 June 2001 in which he describes one of the tasks they undertook:

> . . . the early conditions in the camp were abysmal, particularly the water supply which was so poor, that vessels of every shape and kind had to be left under the few taps available in order to ensure the bare requirements of cooking and minimal hygiene purposes. The water main was in the road alongside the area marked as 'Canal' (see plan) although this was actually one of the smaller docks on the outskirts of the main harbour. As the Japanese guardroom was the furthest away from the source and supplied with just one $1/2$" tap, their daytime supply often petered out by midday due to the demands in the camp where, at one time, there were 4500 prisoners. We in the Royal Engineers Workshop (marked R.E., adjacent to Sunset Gate – top right) therefore had little difficulty in persuading our captors to allow us to improve the situation. This we did by getting them to commandeer a quantity of 2" diameter galvanised pipes from the Docks Authority, which I connected to an outside fire hydrant located near the Japanese billets (marked by dotted line to left of centre). I was then able to furnish each compound with a separate water supply and subsequently, by dint of recycling salvaged plumbing from nearby abandoned houses, was able to provide much needed showers and the means of regular flushing to the new drainage system that we had laid down. It will also interest you to know that I made a tubular bed from some of the surplus 2" pipe for our CO Col. Humphries. Two of our Signals technicians then built a miniature radio set which was concealed in one of the bed legs. This was operated by Colonel Humphries, using a single earphone and a concealed wire under his pillow, also further concealed by his mosquito net.

Opposite:
This plan was drawn in 1942 by Captain Duncan at the beginning of his book, *Java, Jeopardy and Jail*. The additional information – dotted lines and notes – were added by John Baxter in 2001.

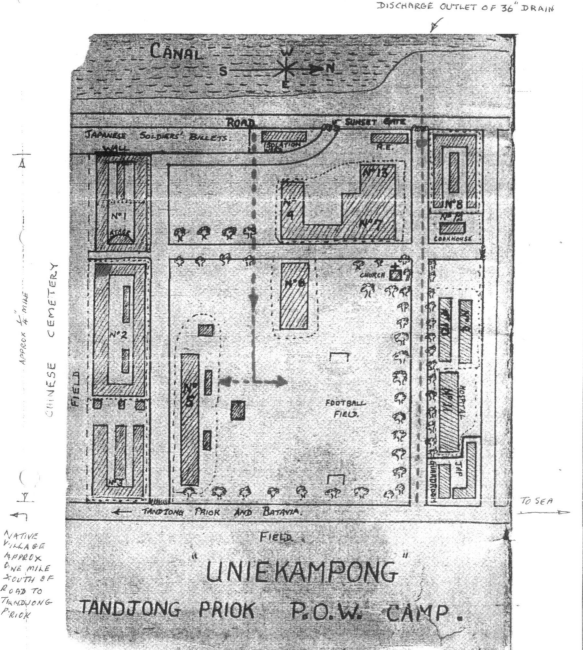

DISCHARGE OUTLET OF 36" DRAIN

CANAL

JAPANESE SOLDIERS' BILLETS

ROAD SUNSET GATE

ISOLATION

WALL

R.E.

Nº1

Nº13

Nº4

Nº7

Nº8

Nº12

COOKHOUSE

CHINESE CEMETERY

FIELD

Nº2

Nº6

CHURCH

Nº10

Nº9

HOSPITAL

Nº11

Nº5

FOOTBALL FIELD.

GUARDROOM

TRAP

Nº3

← TANDJONG PRIOK AND BATAVIA.

TO SEA →

APPROX ¼ MILE

NATIVE
VILLAGE
APPROX
ONE MILE
SOUTH OF
ROAD TO
TANDJONG
PRIOK

FIELD.

"UNIE KAMPONG"

TANDJONG PRIOK P.O.W. CAMP.

FORESHORE OF SEA (APPROX ¼ MILE) FOOD WAS COOKED IN SEA WATER FOR ITS SALT CONTENT

THIS AREA WAS FORMERLY A HOUSING ESTATE, ABANDONED BY DUTCH RESIDENTS
AFTER CAPITULATION.

BOUNDARY OF CHINESE CEMETERY

KEY {

←----------→ LINE OF 2" WATER MAIN (BEFORE FINAL CONNECTIONS TO HUTS)

– – – – – LINE OF 36" UNDERGROUND DRAIN (SEE MANHOLE NEAR R.E. W/SHOP)

In contrast to the wiring-off of the camp, this work was carried out to the highest professional standard, given the circumstances prevailing, and many of the inmates, Dad included, owed their lives to the work done by these men.

I recently had the pleasure of meeting John and could thank him personally for all his help and encouragement. He has added greatly to my understanding and knowledge of the camp. When I had sent him a copy of Dad's plan of the layout of Tandjong Priok camp he had been very impressed with the accuracy and attention to detail. He carefully marked on the plan details of the work carried out by the engineers including the planned breaches in the perimeter fence, the outlying settlements as well as detailed plans of the new drainage and water supply work. I am very grateful to him for sharing this information and for his patient understanding of my need to find out more.

Back to spring 1942 and the Japanese commandant wasted little time in laying down the rules of the camp: no escape attempts, no radios and no keeping of diaries or journals. With such large numbers of prisoners, the Japanese left them to organise themselves. In the case of the British forces this was quickly established, the senior officer in Dad's section being Major Whiting, who had been Officer Commanding, 2nd Echelon in General Sitwell's HQ. He now issued the following orders to his section (see opposite).

The cartoon (on page 62), which I believe was drawn by Dad, was found among his papers and sums it up rather neatly.

The men were quickly organised into working parties on the docks (see page 11). John Baxter recalls that this was 'the largest of the docks, capable of handling liners and large coasters. The dockside warehouses suffered much bomb damage . . . the general view is much as I remember it.'

The men in these dock parties were supervised by their own officers who were used as forced labour too, contrary to all conventions. They were required to work long hours both day and night initially clearing bomb damage in and around the dockside warehouses, or godowns as they were known locally. Once this work was done the prisoners were involved in building repair-work and loading ships bound for Japan and the various theatres of war in and around the East Indies. At least there were some benefits as the stores and supplies they were loading could be plundered to supplement rations back in camp.

The notebook that he wrote his diary entries in was a small pocket book, the inside front cover of which had the signatures of several close friends, among whom is Lieutenant Derrick Montgomery-Campbell (see page 63). Derrick, together with Steve Day, Des Campion, Dennis Glasgow and Atholl were all on the run in Java. They called themselves The Five Aces.

G.H.Q. ORDERS
by
MAJOR WHITING.

No. 1.   24.4.42.

1. MORNING ROLL CALL will take place 5 mins. after REVEILLE.

2. With effect from to-day all officers and men will arise at Reveille,
    only men who have been detailed by the M.O. will remain in bed.

3. MORNING INSPECTION. All ranks below that of Sergeant will parade
    at 8.30 a.m. for inspection, washed, shaved and suitably attired.

4. N.C.O's i/c rooms and men occupying small rooms will ensure that
    their room has been scrubbed and all kit is packed as per barrack
    room before the inspection by Major Whiting, Officer Commanding,
    G.H.Q. at 10.30 hrs. daily. Also that that portion of verandah
    and drain in the immediate vicinity of room is washed and cleaned.

5. PHYSICAL TRAINING. All officers and men under 35 years of age
    excepting those excused by M.O. or engaged on essential duties will
    parade at 10.30 a.m. for physical training. Failure to comply with
    this order will result in disciplinary action being taken against
    offendor.

6. BATMEN. As from to-day no man will fulfill duties as batman for
    more than one officer. L/Cpl. Boyden will be N.C.O. i/c Batmen
    and all requests, complaints etc. will be made to him for necessary
    action. Where batmen are desirous of volunteering for fatigue
    parties arrangements for their duties to be performed by another
    batman must be made with the officers concerned the night pevious.

7. OBSCENE LANGUAGE. The use of obscene language in barrack rooms
    will cease forthwith.

8. URINATING. The practice of urinating into drains or through the
    barbed wire surrounding No. 1.Camp is to cease forthwith. Action
    will be taken against any offender committing these offences.

9. PARADES. It has been noticed that members of G.H.Q. do not exhibit
    the usual promptness or smartness when answering roll calls or parading
    for duty, from to-day onwards disciplinary action will be taken
    against all.persons who fail to act in a prompt and soldier like manner.

10. COMPLAINTS. Complaints will be made in writing and signed and handed
    to W.O. II. Roberts, and will be given every consideration. Those of
    a frivolous or trivial nature will NOT be accepted.

11. RETREAT. "Retreat" will be sounded at 19.45 hrs. daily and will serve
    as a signal for those outside camp to return by 20.00 hrs. On hearing
    this call all men will stand at "attention" irrespective of place or
    nature of work.

12. EVENING ROLL CALL. Roll call will take place at 20.05 hrs.

13. LECTURES. Those persons desirous of attending or giving lectures
    or talks, technical or topical please hand particulars etc. to
    W.O. II. Roberts.

2.

14. CLASSES. It has been suggested that classes be held for those wishing to improve their knowledge of various subjects. Will those willing to instruct and those wishing to attend please hand their particulars to W.O. II. Roberts.

15.   Message to Officers and all ranks from Major Whiting, Officer Commanding, G.H.Q.

        "It is my wish that all men endeavour to uphold the traditions of the British Army by observing the following:-

1. Respect for senior and junior ranks.
2. Bearing of indignities in the true British manner.
3. Full co-operation between all ranks.
4. Maintain a soldier like manner at all times bearing in mind that release will eventually be effected and above all no "dog - in - the - manger " spirit is requested or required but what I would like to see is "chins up, thumbs up and a permanent smile".

16. ORDER OF THE DAY.

BATHING.   In view of the conditions under which we are at present compelled to live and the climate and general conditions prevalant in this part of the world it is most essential that all personnel bath at least once daily, therefore with effect from to-day all members of G.H.Q. will bath between 18.30 and 20.00 hrs. Arrangements are being made for a large can as bath to be erected, in the meantime use must be made of utensils etc. available.

                                              MAJOR,
                          Officer Commanding, G. H. Q.

Chins up, thumbs up, and a permanent smile: the cartoon in response to Major Whiting's Orders, found in the diary.

Inside front cover of Java notebook.

Opened diary pages.

The diary extract on page 1 covers those 11 days from 8–19 March 1942 when the five of them, joined by others, enjoyed their last days of freedom.

Picking up the diary for April-May 1942 a month after his arrival in camp, he recounts events as follows:

1942

April 28th   *Nasty dose of fever. Dant lent me his camp bed. Bought mosquito net f4.50 Whiting and his tar-paint rather got us down. Dock party searched. No seaplanes for some days.*

April 29th   *Felt better today. Very young Jap troops landed yesterday. Motley ill-equipped mob landed today. Alleged to have said that troops are being moved out of Japan due to food shortage. Not very likely. Also that Turkey had come in on our side.*

April 30th   *Turkey rumour false. Fever again last night.*

1st May   *Prisoners accommodated in two jails in Batavia. Discipline very strict. 4 shot trying to escape. 5 died due to spinal meningitis! Hospital conditions in Batavia atrocious. No beds, no supplies and operations performed without anaesthetic.*

2nd May   *Death in camp hospital from dysentry.*

3rd May   *Down with fever and poisoned arm.*

4th–7th May   *Nothing of importance. Lot of shipping in. Aircraft active.*

8th May   *Rumours that allied plane flew over at great height. On dock fatigue. N.B.G. Two more deaths in hospital at Batavia.*

10th May   *Church as usual AA guns practice 50 Javanese released by japs. T.S.F. indifferent of late.*

11th May   *Other arm poisoned. Another death in hospital.*

12th May   *2nd issue of cheese today. Japs getting nasty about our buying stores. Star gazes still going strong.*

13th May   *Rice sweepings for breakfast.*

14th May   *American, Dutch and Australian troops moved to Batavia. British troops from jail to here.*

15th May   *Col. Russell made bog up with Japs. Turned out at 1am for count.*

Mentions of the radio and church appear regularly and are an indication of the importance of both in his life at that time. The 'book' he refers to was the story of the time he and Des Campion spent in Java which they decided to write with a view publishing one day. It filled one whole notebook and was completed during the next year or so, *Java, Jeopardy and Jail* being the title that they chose.

Among Dad's letters is one dated 18 December 1951 written by Des Campion who by that time was married and living in Bristol. In it he mentions two of the characters who shared their experiences in Java before captivity and in camp. One of them, Alan Dant, is referred to in the diary entry for 28 April. The other is Steve Day, one of the Five Aces. Des passed on recent information about the two:

'. . . Do you remember Steve Day and Alan Dant in Tandjong Priok? I saw Steve in June 1950 with his wife when they were in England on holiday from Batavia, where Steve is still working. Alan and his wife are on leave from Sarawak at the moment and spent last weekend with us. They come home for six months every three years . . .'

The notebook survived but the story was never published. How did this and the rest of his collection survive? Well, apart from sheer luck, one thing that he did early on during the few weeks they were on the run in Java, was to have the foresight to swap his British kitbag for a Dutch one. The reason for this was that Dutch bags were double-lined and when the seam in the lining was split open a useful pocket was created in which could be hidden notebooks and other precious items. He was indeed lucky that his kitbag didn't go missing on the numerous occasions that they were moved around, nor was it seriously interfered with when it was kept in the store rooms in each camp, despite having some things stolen from it. It was also a matter of luck that he was never searched thoroughly. The following extract written towards the end of his captivity describes the lengths to which he had to go to conceal his precious record:

. . . the Japs tightened their supervision of us, and as diaries were strictly forbidden and confiscated if found, I had to conceal the existing manuscripts by sewing them into the lining of clothes, under false bottoms in my packs and in other ways . . .

In view of the brevity of diary entries for the early period in captivity, it is useful to draw on the narrative *Java, Jeopardy and Jail* to explain some of the more interesting episodes during this time. One such account is the story of how the Australian engineers built a church inside the camp.

Not long after we arrived at Priok, it was suggested that a small chapel should be built as there was plenty [of] wood in the camp as well as cement, the skilled labour and architects were all there too, so the Japanese were approached with a request that a small church might be erected, the reply being 'yes' on the condition that the Japs were not called upon to supply any materials other than those already present. The site that was chosen was at one end of the football pitch where locust trees with their scarlet blossom and overhanging shady foliage provided shelter from the blazing heat of the tropical sun, and work was begun early in April 1942. The walls of the chapel were made of reinforced concrete with the north side left open in the shape of a gothic arch whilst the south wall had two windows let into it which were later to contain stained glass designs incorporating the figure of St George of England and the flags of all the nationalities of the prisoners in Priok; inside the chapel itself there was an altar covered with sarong cloth and carved wood candlesticks on each side of a crucifix, teak wood polished with talcum powder and brown boot polish being used for the altar and its fittings. Outside, a concrete pulpit was erected and small shrubs, palms and flowers were planted all round the chapel and pulpit whilst the grass in front was cut short. Every Sunday, weather permitting service was held at 10am and the . . .

congregation led by a choir sang popular psalms and hymns and then listened to a short sermon by either of our two padres, the Rev. Harper-Holcroft and the Rev. Phillips. Both the padres were excellent men for the job and would preach a short sermon which everybody could understand bringing out points that they had noticed during the previous week whilst going around the sub-camps. In addition to the service, communion was held every Sunday

at 8 A.M. & 11 A.M. and a Toc H
group held meetings in the evening.
There was a serene charm about the
whole of the chapel area which was not to
be found anywhere else in the camp
and I used to look forward to the
service each week as a great source
of spiritual comfort. Not long before
we left Java, a dedication notice
in carved wood was added to the
chapel, this reading as follows:-
"This church was erected by English and
Australian Prisoners of War in Tandjong Priok

Camp to the glory of God, and as a memorial
to those who lived, to those who suffered, to
those who died there during the Nipponese
occupation of Java, and to the unconquerable
spirit of the Allies."
The church was dedicated to St. George of
England by the Rev. R.H. Harper-Holcroft
Chaplain to the Forces, July 1942.

The carved wooden dedication notice did not survive but in 1961 a
permanent memorial to the building of St George's chapel was erected in a
church in Jakarta (see back cover).

Captain Duncan helped in this project by collecting scrap glass which was then used to make two stained glass windows. As has already been said, prisoners were put to work clearing bomb damage in the area and coloured glass was in plentiful supply both around the camp and on the docks. An appeal went out from Lieutenant Commander Upton (a naval officer closely involved with the church project) to anyone on outside working parties to bring back pieces of coloured glass with which to make the windows.

Amazingly, these windows have survived and are a permanent reminder of the power of faith in such adversity.

1996

During late December 1996, I visited my parents' home frequently. Mum was exhausted and looked unwell but she refused to see a doctor so my sisters and I did all we could to help out. Dad had rallied and during the evenings I spent time with him listening carefully as he reminisced about his war. Looking back, it seemed as though he wanted to 'hand over' and so I resumed the task of transcribing the diaries, a job which was by then over half way to completion. He took a keen interest and was only too willing to clarify points ensuring that I had understood correctly.

As we looked through the many cuttings he'd kept from the English language propaganda newspapers which had circulated in the camps, Dad happened upon one which was particularly significant for him. Torn from a copy of the *Nippon Times* dated Sunday 23 June 1943, it showed a group of men beside a church.

'I was there when they took that,' he said. 'It was the day of the consecration of the chapel which was built by the prisoners.' Fascinated, I took a closer look. 'How did you get hold of this?' I asked. He told me that by a strange coincidence he had found the article, published over a year after the photograph had been taken, just after he had arrived at Zentsuji (the second camp he was sent to in Japan). He described what it had meant to him and the other prisoners to have such a fine building as the focal point for their weekly worship. It was strange but also comforting to hear him talking like that, he had never shared his feelings in this way before.

He could vividly remember two of the padres in camp, though there were others. Harper-Holdcroft was the older and more pious man; the Reverend Phillips was younger and Dad found he related to him better. I asked if the church had survived but he didn't think it had. However, he believed that the windows still existed as an Australian ex-POW friend had told him that they had been saved and were kept in a church somewhere in Jakarta.

New Year 1997 came and went and was a very subdued affair for us all. A couple of days later I was back at work and my good friend with whom I shared an office, asked about my Christmas. I broke down as I recalled how

NIPPON TIMES, SUN

Chapel in the Open

The considerate treatment of the war prisoners in Java by the Military Administration there may be gauged by the freedom given in religious matters. Prisoners who profess the Christian religion are allowed to hold and attend a service every Sunday. The picture shows a chapel in the open, ami pleasant surroundings, with some of the pri in the middle of a service.

(Passed by the War Ministry)

Cutting from *The Nippon Times*, 23 June 1943, featuring the story of the consecration of the chapel. The Reverend Harper-Holdcroft right of centre with the Reverend Phillips far right seated at the piano. Dad was in the congregation behind the camera.

events had unfolded. Lyn tried to comfort me, listening patiently and asking if there was anything she could do to help. I calmed down and made arrangements with her to take time off in the coming weeks so that I could help my sister look after Dad at home.

It is said that, 'God moves in mysterious ways . . .' and I would have to say that what followed certainly reinforced my belief in that. It suddenly came to me. Yes, there was something she could do to help, could she ask her husband (who was a curate) if he could look up in Crockford's Directory and find the name of an Anglican Bishop, or Archbishop (I really wasn't fussy!) in Indonesia. Her quizzical look elicited an explanation about the chapel and its windows. I desperately wanted to try and find them for Dad before it was too late.

Instead of her husband she rang her son, Peter, who was an architect working for a large Australian firm and at that time was based in Kuala Lumpur. She got him on the second attempt and having sketched in the details, asked if they had an office in Jakarta. Bingo! He gave her the name and fax number of a friend of his, Matthew Tregale, who worked there. I then hurriedly drafted a brief note outlining my quest and faxed it off to this unsuspecting young man on the other side of the world.

That was on Friday 3 January, 1997. I heard nothing for five days but then on the 8th I was in the office when a fax came through from Jakarta. Matthew had been on leave and on his return to the office that morning had read my message. He would see what he could do but wasn't optimistic in view of the vast amount of re-development work that had gone on in the city.

The following day, the 9th and by coincidence my birthday, I was in the office when the fax machine whirred into action again . . . (see opposite).

I couldn't believe my eyes. I felt so elated, but it wasn't to last very long. Literally within minutes of reading the fax the telephone rang and it was my sister, in tears, asking me to come straight away to my parents' house, as she'd just had more bad news. I left the office immediately to begin the longest six weeks of my life.

Mum was in heart failure and needed to be admitted to hospital straight away. I accompanied her in the ambulance and later that day we learnt that she also had a tumour in her lung (in due course it transpired that she had lymphoma). Three days after Mum's admission Dad, who had rallied for a little while, suddenly collapsed having suffered another gastric haemorrhage. He was admitted to a ward at the opposite end of the third floor of the same hospital that Mum was in. I will never forget the sunset that Mum and I watched from her room that afternoon. It developed suddenly and grew across the horizon to engulf the whole sky. It was quite simply breathtakingly beautiful, glorious in the intensity of the vivid colours. It seemed to be a portent – I desperately hoped of calmer and more reassuring times. When I got back home that evening, the photographs had arrived.

I was up very early the following morning and saw a dawn which I can only

Fax dated 9 January 1997 informing me that Matthew had found the windows.

DATE : 09 JANUARY 1997

RE :

Number of pages including this one : 3 (Three)

Dear Meg,

Good news - we've found your Father's windows.

There are in fact two windows which have been framed and prominently mounted on the rear wall of the All Saints Anglican Church in Central Jakarta. Each window is approximately 200 mm wide x 1000 mm high. Beneath is a plaque which reads as follows :

THESE WINDOWS
WERE IN A CHAPEL AT TANDJUNG PRIOK
BUILT BY PRISONERS OF WAR IN 1942

THEY WERE PAINTED BY
LIEUTENANT COMMANDER H.C. UPTON R.N.V.R.
NOW CHIEF ARCHITECT OF
CABLE AND WIRELESS LIMITED LONDON

THIS PLAQUE HAS BEEN PRESENTED BY
CABLE AND WIRELESS LIMITED
IN MEMORY OF ALLIED SERVICEMEN
WHO DIED IN JAVA

FEBRUARY 1961

I visited the church this morning and fired off two rolls of film. The Church was very dark and I was reluctant to use flash as I was concerned about reflections so we actually took the windows down from the wall and also photographed them outside in the sunlight. I was afraid that the windows would not photograph very well and shot off a range of shots with different exposures and also took some partial close up shots to show greater detail.

The Minister of the Church is an Australian, The Reverend Allen W.Quee (name card attached) but he doesn't have any knowledge of the altar or the candlesticks. However, he remembers a visit of ten or so Australian ex POW's two years ago who were visiting the war cemetery here and who also tracked down the windows. He tells an extremely moving story of one gentlemen standing staring at the windows with tears streaming down his face. Unfortunately he has no idea of their names or how to contact them.

My own father is 77 years old and also served during the second world war with the British Army. I know that sometimes he views the world with despair and asks himself what it was all for. Standing in front of the windows in church this morning I was deeply moved at the sacrifice people like our fathers made (many with their lives) which enables us to enjoy our world today - a sacrifice which is all too often forgotten. When I received your fax yesterday I have to admit I held little hope of finding anything after so long. The fact that the windows have not only survived but have been preserved in excellent condition and occupy pride of place in the church is a powerful indication that their sacrifice has not been forgotten

With best wishes to you and your father

Matthew Tregale

describe as being spectacular, a vivid match for the previous evening's sunset. Later, I took the photographs in to give to Dad. The expression on his face was wonderful.

He couldn't believe it, as he stared at the photographs of the windows after all that time. It meant so much to him to know that these windows, and what they represented to him and the thousands of others who had shared Tandjong Priok, were honoured and remembered still. He read Matthew's fax with its transcript of Lieutenant Commander Upton's plaque. This is placed alongside the windows where they hang on the end wall of the Anglican Church of All Saints, Jakarta, either side of the font – that most potent symbol of new life.

He was so pleased to have the pictures to add to his collection and he told me to contact Matthew straight away and tell him that a large whisky awaited him if ever he was to visit our neck of the woods. I'm still hoping to provide that sustenance one day.

More recently I have come across two other women who had an interest in the church. The first, Lesley Clark, I had made contact with her through a website for COFEPOW – an organisation for children and families of Far Eastern prisoners of war. She was searching for information about Tandjong Priok where her father had also been a prisoner.

This charitable organisation was set up in 1997 by Carol Cooper, another daughter of a prisoner of war. One of its aims is to help the children and families of ex-prisoners of war in their search to find out more about the experiences of their relatives. Lesley's father, William (Bill) Ellmore, RA, like so many other Far Eastern prisoners, had never spoken about his wartime. He had died a few years earlier, and among the few items that he left pertaining to this time was a drawing of St George's chapel. Lesley sent me a copy of this sketch which had been drawn by his friend Geoff Tyson. I reciprocated with copies of Dad's plan of the camp, the news cutting and photographs of the windows, together with one or two extracts from his diaries describing that time in his captivity.

The second, Heather Godfrey, I got in touch with after following a rather circuitous route which started when Mr Suddaby (at the Imperial War Museum) gave me the name of another person researching some of the same camps that I had an interest in. The Reverend John Bliss had visited his office only the week before I did in 1998. He lives in the USA and was researching details about his father's prisoner of war experiences. We corresponded at that time and he told me that he was hoping to meet up with another of the padres from Tandjong Priok, Reverend Rupert Godfrey, who lived in East Anglia. More recently during my research for this book, I re-read this correspondence and picking up on the information about Reverend Godfrey I once again turned to Crockford's for help, this time through my local library. He was listed and so I decided to get in touch.

The two painted glass windows which had originally been behind the the altar of St George's chapel, Tandjong Priok prisoner of war camp.

Matthew Tregale taking the photographs outside All Saints Anglican Church in Jakarta, January 1997.

Drawing of St George's chapel done by Bill Ellmore's friend, Geoff Tyson.

I spoke to Heather, his wife, who told me that her husband had died in 1997. She remembered John Bliss, who had visited them, though sadly her husband was too ill to meet him at the time. She was interested in my search and told me that she and her son would soon be publishing her husband's records (I look forward to being able to read more about him one day).

Just a few weeks after that conversation, I went to visit her at home in Suffolk. I am grateful to her for her warm welcome and generous spirit in sharing so much of her husband's experiences with me. She, like myself and so many of the people I have come into contact with during my research, shares the same belief that our relatives' experiences should not be hidden away and forgotten. Her husband, like Dad and Lesley's father, could not share what happened to him very easily. None of them wished to re-visit those times which were so full of suffering. But they have so much to teach us about the human spirit, the will to survive.

The thing I will remember most from our meeting was walking into her cosy sitting room on that sunny afternoon and coming face to face with another drawing of St George's chapel, Tandjong Priok. Viewed from a different angle than the other two images I have seen, it was still instantly recognisable, and is signed by the artist and dated 1943. She didn't know about the windows having survived and when I got home I sent her some copies of the photographs I had. I am pleased that Dad's records can be shared in this way, I know that is what he would have done.

1942

May–August 8th   *Nothing of very great import during this period. Many rumours about our being shipped from Java etc. but mostly wishful thinking for foundation. Nips allow us a canteen and have issued cigars!!! During this period my spirits have bobbed up and down pretty regularly. At times I felt quite happy but at other [times] have known deepest despair. Elizabeth and folks at home constantly in my thoughts and I long for this war to end so that I can get back to those so near and dear to me. Sickness in the camp has been on the increase more than 50% being on the sick list, myself being one, having had another recurrence of malaria – my ninth attack – which was promptly followed by tonsillitis. My nerves have deteriorated and I am inclined to be sarcastic and bad tempered, whilst small things cause me intense annoyance – Steve's voice and manners on occasion rousing me to a fury . . .*

He recognised the change in himself and when I read this passage it struck a chord with me too. However, despite such irritations and difficulties some of the prisoners didn't lose their ability to appreciate rare moments of beauty, which is illustrated by the following account.

During that summer in camp, one of the young Scottish soldiers (an OR – other rank – in his section) died and his personal effects were given to Captain Duncan for safe-keeping until they could be returned to the young man's family. Among the pitifully few reminders of this man's life, and wretched end, was a folded piece of paper on which was written a vivid snapshot of the world around him in camp entitled 'Sunset Gate'. It was signed with the initials JVM, all that remained of the young man's identity. Dad could so readily identify with the sentiments and so moved was he by the beauty of the prose, that he copied it out into the front of a new notebook for safe keeping (see p. 76).

Three years later, a little while after his homecoming, Captain Duncan ensured that the few items belonging to the young man were returned to his family.

The next few entries are worth recording for they give further insight into Dad's character, his reliance on past experiences and interests, his sense of humour and depth of faith. He was not averse to showing the 'good' side of the Japanese character, on the rare occasions it showed itself. This was also the first time he commented on medical staff: it became increasingly obvious the influence that this group were to have on the sick young man.

Sunset Gate.

Every night between a quarter to & eight o'clock, you see them gather at the gateway, (now barb-wired off) where we made our original never-to-be-forgotten entrance to this camp. At first, only a few men could be seen standing by the fence, but as the nights have gone by, the numbers have increased. For the most part there is little conversation. They just stand and look — and think. At what are they looking and about what are they thinking, these silent men.

The gateway overlooks a dock basin where ships are moored to landing stages. Is that the attraction? Are they thinking of the day when they will walk through the gate as free men, board a similar ship and sail for home. The gateway faces due west. Are they thinking of their families and friends who are so far away in that direction? Perhaps these thoughts are running through their minds. I know they often are in mine as I stand there. But to many the chief attraction of this west end gateway must be the glorious sunsets, sunsets unlike any to be seen in Scotland (glorious as they are on many occasions.)

Nightly above the silhouette of the dockla

with its warehouses, coaling gantries, cranes and masts nature provides a kaleidescope of colour which changes every few seconds as the sun sinks quickly over the horizon. Storm clouds catch & hold, for a brief period, the final rays as they sweep upwards, and hazy films of cloud cap them with a golden mist - forming a dream range of mountains. The scene changes & the sky becomes a beautiful egg-shell blue (a blue such as I have never seen at home) which gradually deepens in tone as darkness quickly falls.

The show is over for another night - another day nearer freedom - and as we turn from Sunset Gate to walk back to camp we can ponder on the fact that, before we see it again, the sun, which has given us such a beautiful few minutes, will have provided a glorious June day for our loved ones at home.

— J. V. M.

Tandjong Priok Prison Camp
Java 1942.

August 9th   *Meant to get up today – been in bed for 16 days now but felt very weak, so stayed put. New doc came round, had been at Glasgow and knew W. Bridges, called Dr Barclay, seems a good chap. John Lambert, our "quack", has been very kind and has done a great deal for me – whilst I was sick. Wish to heaven we could get out but expect will be here for some time yet. Always maintained that release would come about Xmas or New Year. With things as they are do not hold much hope of getting out by then now. Nips now getting air-raid conscious and have laid down routine for same. Glorious smell of cooking coming from the fireplace where some OR's are stewing up some beanstalk pods from the trees to extract sugar content. Bemoan the loss of the camera these days as several good subjects in here. Day is a noisy sod.*

Aug. 10th–20th   *Have been feeling much more optimistic of late. Probably due to T.S.F. which has been V.V.G. There always is so much that I want to do and yet I do not have the mental concentration to get down to anything. Somehow, all my energies seem to have gone for all I do is read and brew cups of tea. Maj. Petrie often drops round and we chat about "Bonnie Scotland" for hours on end. Elizabeth and the folks at home seem so near and yet so far and while I often think about our re-union, it too often seems to be a very pleasant dream which buoys one up and yet has no real basis. However, some day we are going to re-unite for I know that they are all praying for my safety just as I pray for theirs and am quite prepared to accept His gracious will. It is funny how one's faith grows strong on occasions like these. Well, here's to Xmas in Australia and Easter in Scotland. Still feel very weak but daily I am picking up. Find the Nips idea of ARP rather amusing and hope that some day very soon the sounding of the siren will have some real significance. Usual crop of rumours about (1) our moving (2) Nips moving and (3) Allied activities.*

Aug 21st–29th   *Steady improvement in my health. Am now getting iron tonic and cod liver oil and eggs and Vit B tablets, Maj. Petrie having supplied CLO and Vit B. Malignant malaria very much on increase and has taken a heavy toll. Two lads went out from Camp 3 and were caught by native police in TP. All camps aroused at 2330hrs and kept on parade for*

1¹/₂hrs. Pace and Ordly offcr given 15 days in solitary and camp 5 days fatigues. Lads taken to Batavia and have not yet returned. At last concert in No. 5 camp Nip Sgt. Maj. came to see the show and was given a stool which promptly collapsed when he sat on it, his nibs going arse over tip into a nearby drain. Yells of laughter from the audience!!! Nip took it in good part and joined in the laugh. T.S.F. has much improved of late. Nips moving troops and stores from the island. Rumour that marines are taking over.

Aug 30–31st   Feeling a great deal better these days. Have been thinking of home and the folks probably far too much than is good for my mental outlook but no matter what I do, thoughts of home keep cropping up. Have decided that nothing on God's earth will induce me to stay in the army after the war. Doc Barclay gave me the good news that in view of my malaria I would be sent home when we were released from here. Certainly am fed up with the tropics and as for the Glamour of the East, well . . .

Sept. 1st–7th   Have gone down with another attack of malaria. This is getting beyond a joke now as it is my tenth relapse. Our orchestra is coming on very well these days and it's such a relief to hear some music. As I lie in bed my thoughts often wander back to those happy days when there was no war and I was free to go where I wished. I can still visualise all my favourite fishing pools and long for a walk out the Kinkell Braes when the hyacinths are in full bloom and to smell the soft fragrance of the spring air. Wonder when I shall do that again. Maj. Petrie taken off to Batavia Hospital with beri-beri. Had the bad luck to break a tooth; not sore at the moment but hope it gives no trouble as we have no dentist in camp.

In his book, *Not Much of a Picnic*, John Baxter described being in hospital in Batavia too, occupying the bed next to General Wavell's ADC. Perhaps this was Major Petrie, a view which seems to be corroborated by John's recollections:

' . . . it could certainly have been Major Petrie who was my bedside companion as I remember he was of that rank and the dates coincide with the time I spent in 'hospital' (I use inverted commas because it was a school of botany, taken over by the Japanese for prisoners of war). I am afraid my memory does not stretch to knowing his surname, we spent a very limited time together before I returned to camp, leaving him behind . . . My sum knowledge of my discussion with him was confined to his reference to being left behind in Bandoeng to destroy all military records, after Wavell and other members of his staff had flown back to India when the Japanese invaded Java.'

This last detail certainly fitted with my father's recollections of events. In *Java, Jeopardy and Jail* Dad tells another story which highlights the contrasts that he experienced while a prisoner. The account opposite illustrates a welcome reminder of life at home (the family had always been besotted with cats). I can well imagine the comfort that these wild animals must have brought to him in that place, and the effect that caring for something so defenceless must have had on his emotional well-being.

The next few entries make interesting reading as they include mentions of the pigeons, the story that had impressed Mr Suddaby.

Sept 14th   *Big events today. My guess that those leaving would be going on a ship has proved correct for they were embarked on the transport along with 1,000 armed Nips. A certain Cpl. in No. 3 camp has been breeding pigeons and when Russell and co left they took two birds with them (one brooding) and so far one has returned with the news. This is about the smartest thing that has been done up to date. It also appears that we are to get injections tomorrow. As the grip the bird brought back stated a 3 day boat journey Sumatra would appear to be their destination. I personally do not think they are going to Malaya for there they would need nets and in any case, the Nips must have food difficulties. Of course Korea or Formosa is not out of the question and would also account for our injections as fire and disease are their two bete noires. Still, time will tell. Crafter thinks invasion should come this week.*

Sept 16th   *A further party of 300 has been embarked today, this time they were taken from the jail, so it looks as if we are all going to be moved sooner or later. Have started to make a small model of a Swordfish and so far it has been quite successful. John Lambert tells me that I got the last of the plasmogin in the area so I hope I get no more relapses. Day was on working party and went 35 miles on the other side of Batavia. Said the natives were jeering at them along the route. Food, of late, has been pretty awful and am very thankful for the eggs I can get – at 6ct each!! – As I write this,*

I had managed to tame a small cat that used to come round the wire looking for something to eat by feeding it with odd scraps of food and, as time passed, it used to appear in my billet at every mealtime and meow until it had been ~~feed~~ fed; the only drawback was that it was a female and it soon became apparent that before long I was going to be the possessor of not one cat but several, ~~and I~~ but my fears that either my bed or my room was going to be ~~used for it~~ selected for the happy event proved groundless as she vanished for about three days and then reappeared carrying a kitten in her mouth, dumped it in my room on some empty sandbags I had put there for the purpose and then went off and brought the remaining one. They were a beautiful pair of kittens and I christened them

"Big" and "Stinker" not because either of them were, but because they afforded me about as much entertainment as their human namesakes had done in days gone by. A few weeks later just when they had reached the fluffy and frisky stage, one of them climbed up inside Capt. Maclean's mosquito net when he was lying asleep and fell onto his head, waking him up with a yell. I do not know who was more startled as he thought it was a rat but the kitten shot into my room at top speed and darted under the table where it remained for quite a long time.

Story about the cat and kittens from the notebook *Java, Jeopardy & Jail*.

Elizabeth's photo is before me and I wonder when I shall see her again. Expect she is Dr Glassey by now, bless her precious heart.

Sept 17th   Sgt. Maj. Roberts gave me his silver cigarette case today; it is rather a beautiful affair. Nothing of interest otherwise.

Sept 18th   T.S.F. very discouraging. Rumour has it that our Nip guards are leaving on the 20th and that the Wog police are taking over with the present Commandant i/c. To my mind this is bad news as the Wogs will make the most of their new found authority. Also the new hospital is supposed to be going to be used for a kids school run on 'Asia for the Asiatics' principle; which to me is also a bad thing.

Sept 19th–20th   Great activity down at the Nip Guardroom. They have burned all records and have moved out all the furniture and kept Camp No. 9 up all night with the row they made boozing. Two white Dutch kids came up to the wire and gave us a present of tobacco. Contrary to rumour, our new guards are Nips and are very young and zealous, having patrolled up and down the wire all afternoon whilst the bath party were searched on their return to camp . . . First pay parade, rates being officers 25ct, W.O.'s 2 and Sgts 15ct, Cpls. and under 10ct. Model progressing favourably. T.S.F.N.B.G. New hospital used as billet.

Sept 21st   These new guards are a set of bastards. Good concert but was rather spoiled by the presence of two of above who kept slapping people. Great shakes at night as rumour has it that most of Camps 1 & 2 are being shipped away on Wednesday. If true this probably means the parting of the ways for the 3 Aces as I am still SIQ (sick in quarters).

22nd Sept   Once again rumour has proved correct for Camps 1 & 2 are moving at 5pm tonight. Everybody of my clique are going but I stay behind. Gave Des the bulk of the stores and got ƒ32.00 from him. Evidently they are going to Borneo. Place like a morgue at night with all the usual gang away. Felt very depressed about the whole business but somehow at the back of my mind I have a feeling that it is all for my own good that I did not go. T.S.F. better today.

Sept 23rd *The emptiness of this camp seems to hit one and it was a great relief to hear one of the band practising 'Tales of Hoffman' on the violin this morning. Spent most of the day cleansing up the bunk and getting things in order. Got my first innoculation this afternoon. Both pigeons back today. Say that 504 gone from jail as well and Borneo supposed to be destination. Russell rumoured to be in Batavia in solitary for having been found with a revolver and ammo in his possession. We are all going to get our heads shaved tomorrow. Nip aircraft doing night landing practice.*

How prophetic the last part of the entry for 22 September was; another example of why later on after the war Dad felt he had been so lucky. He was quite right and given what was later learnt of the fate of many of the prisoners of war in Borneo, Des was extremely lucky to survive.

His reference on 16 September (last two lines) to Elizabeth, 'Expect she is Dr Glassey by now' was a little premature. What he couldn't know, had no way of knowing, was that Elizabeth and his family were also 'captives' in a sense, all of them imprisoned by the same lack of information, isolated in their anxiety and worry for him and in their different ways for each other. There was so little news about the thousands who were missing and no reliable information had been forthcoming from the Japanese. They were so far away.

Back in Dundee, where most of the 5th year medics had finished their final clinical year and were now newly qualified doctors, Elizabeth and her friend Pauline Quig were busy revising again having failed the final medicine paper. They would be able to re-sit the paper in December. Pauline recalled that 'after Singapore fell, Liz seemed to be writing letters almost every day in the hopes that they would reach him'. Then one dreadful day in early summer her letters were returned and it almost broke her heart. However, wallowing in self-pity was never her way and somehow she found the strength to carry on, hoping and praying as did his family, that news would come any day telling them that he was safe and well. It was no wonder that she came down in her finals, the strain was almost unbearable and she would later describe herself as 'almost going mad' during that dreadful time.

His father, an avid and inveterate letter writer in peacetime, was relentless now in his quest for knowledge of his son's whereabouts. He wrote regularly to the War Office asking for information and in late September received the following response:

Tel. No.—Liverpool Wavertree 4000.

Any further communication on this subject should be addressed to :—
The Under-Secretary of State,
The War Office
Casualty Branch,
Blue Coat School,
Church Road,
Wavertree,
Liverpool 15,
and the following number quoted.

NATIONAL SCHEME FOR DISABLED MEN

THE WAR OFFICE
CASUALTY BRANCH,
BLUE COAT SCHOOL,
CHURCH ROAD,
WAVERTREE,
LIVERPOOL 15.

OS/259D (Casualties) 26th September, 1942.

Sir,

With reference to your letter of the 12th September, 1942, I am directed to express regret that no information has been received in this Department regarding your son, Captain A.A. Duncan, The Argyll and Sutherland Highlanders, subsequent to the information that he had arrived in Java and there is no reason to think that he is not still serving there with the British and Allied Forces who are still fighting.

Unfortunately, it is not possible at present to communicate with, or obtain information concerning personnel in Java and it is feared that it may well be some time before any details are known. You may rest assured, however, that any further information received will be passed to you immediately.

I am, Sir,
Your obedient Servant,

A. Williams

A. Duncan, Esq.,
Mansefield,
St. Andrews,
Fife.

The news that he might still be fighting was hardly reassuring as the newsreels reported the Japanese occupation of the Netherlands East Indies.

It must have been so worrying too for her parents back in Bradford for, on the few occasions they did see her, she was so drawn and anxious. Brother Billy, who was by now on active service in HMS *Striker*, and based in New York during that late autumn and Christmas, wrote to his parents trying to encourage their belief that all would be well.

On 18 December both Liz and Pauline heard that they had passed their exams. Mum said many years later, that failing that paper had probably been the best thing that could have happened as she had to focus on her studies and it was in a way a distraction from all the anxiety, though admittedly she didn't see it like that at the time. In January 1943 Dr Elizabeth Glassey started work back home in Bradford as a House Officer at St Luke's, and before long was expected to take on overwhelming responsibility far beyond her experience, though not as it turned out beyond her capabilities.

Back in Tandjong Priok, the last few weeks before the move saw a great deal of activity with prisoners herded both in and out of the camp . . .

Surgeon Lieutenant
W. C. Glassey, RNVR.

Dr J. E. Glassey.

Sept 29th – *Very little doing today. Woke up at 0845hrs but luckily Woten had drawn my breakfast. Washed out the room in the morning. Band concert at night but was not so good as some of late. Rather a sore throat in the evening. Thought about building a small boat and am going to give this more consideration as it has possibilities. Rumour has it that some Aussies are coming to our camp.*

Sept 30th – *Rumour about Aussies true. 150 of them are being landed from a boat and are staying in our camp for 14 days and are then being shipped away again... Spent the morning pottering around and tried to pass the afternoon playing patience but everything I tried came out which was most unsatisfactory. There is one of those yellow swine standing just outside the wire opposite me now shouting at all and sundry to salute him... natives have been making a hell of a row with their tom-toms at night as it is the Fast of Ramedan and all Mohamedans must fast for 30 days i.e. no eating or drinking from sunrise to sunset.*

Oct 1st – Evidently we are going to be paid and will receive the pay of equivalent rank in Jap army. Aussies arrived, and seem not too bad a crowd. Gave a Lt. Nichol quite a feed at night. My tummy has been a bit out of order of late.

Oct 2nd – Verbal skirmish with a Nip today about bowing when inside a room. He came into the camp after me but the gate NCO gave the alarm and I managed to dodge him. Tummy still not so good. Gave Roberts his second French lesson.

Oct 3rd – Got my second cocktail injection today. A few days ago some BF in the RES let a copy of the news fall into Jap hands so now we are without. More forms to fill in. I have a feeling that there are big moves in the air and that we may be shifted in the near future. Had fried egg on toast for supper.

Such indiscreet talk concerning the news, and careless behaviour on occasions by both officers and men, seriously jeopardised the safety of all of them as such news could only have come from a secret radio. More than once the prisoners were extremely lucky to get away with this subterfuge.

Oct 4th – Placed an order with the NAAFI for a case of bully. There is an Aussi dentist in camp so am going to get him to give my mouth the once over.

Oct 5th – Had big eats at night. Made a Nasi Goreng with rice, eggs, onions and bully and was it good. The Aussies are a damn good crowd being 6th battn of the Victorian Scottish. Two of them, Nichol and Duncan Burr, come along quite a lot and have very interesting stories about Timor. Have been feeling quite happy and contented these days and am not worried about prospects of release altho' I still have a hankering to slide over the garden wall one of these days, in spite of the common belief that it would be suicide for I feel that once away from here, you would have nothing much to avoid.

Oct 6th – First rate rain storm last night. Slept inside my flea bag and was not too hot. The small white dog is quite a useful hound at times for he always barks at the Nips and so gives the warning whenever they are around, especially when they come snooping about just outside the wire after dark. No aircraft operating about here at all these days. Terrific rain storm in the evening; in the middle of it, a PB sentry came up the wire so after bowing I positively leered at him and if looks could have killed . . .
Rumour has it that the Yanks have landed at (1) Celibes and (2) New Ireland. Do not believe (1) but think that (2) might possibly be correct.

Oct 7th – Maj. Petrie returned from Batavia. Says the town is dead but plenty of Nips in evidence, but they appear to be on leave. Concert at night. When Roberts was on docks a Dutchman told him the news was good and that we would not be here for long. Native told Plunkett the same story. First Aussie death in camp. He fainted and hit his head on the wall as he fell, fracturing his skull. Nip guards have tamed down considerably of late.

Oct 8th – Had a good laugh about the story of the Christian Scientist who fell overboard at Cape Town. Bully etc came in to the NAAFI today. Woten, my new batman now that Smith has gone . . . Plunkett and Poulton are getting on my nerves these days especially latter who is as mean as they are made, refusing to give away even a cigarette.

Oct 9th – Went along and saw Pace today. He told me about the two RAF who tried to escape and were caught, beaten up, tied to posts just outside the camp and finally shot. Just let those yellow swine wait until our positions are reversed. Had a tremendous feed at night as I had made a Nasi Goreng for supper with all the trimmings so of course the cookhouse had to produce pasties and bread rolls. The local papers say that a Jap ship containing over 1800 British and Aussie POW was torpedoed and sunk in the south China Sea on Oct 1st. This could easily be our party and as only several hundred were saved I hope that it wasn't. Ship called 'Lisbon Maru'.
Oct 10th – Porridge for breakfast today and was it good!!! 650 Aussies arriving at this camp tonight and going away in the morning. Nichol and Co

think that they might be from Ambon. T.S.F. not so bad. Cigarettes are very difficult to obtain these days and a 6ct packet outside costs 35cts in the camp so I am now reduced to smoking wog weed. Have been thinking a good deal of the folks at home of late.

Oct 11th – Mixed body of Dutch, American, Aussi and British troops from Batavia spent last night here. They were issued with woollen underclothing and jackets and are sailing today for Japan or Korea. A Lt. M Humble of US Army bunked with me and left me sundry odds and ends of kit including a pair of shoes and a grip. Brigadier Pearson (viz Singapore, page 45) was slapped by a Jap so promptly slapped him back: Result: Both in the cooler. Not feeling so well today. Listened to the pianist playing Ave Maria etc.

October 12th–13th – Nothing much doing. Was on court martial but found it very boring. Fairish aerial activity of late. Got f10.00 pay from Nips out of f120.00; f60 for board and lodging and f50 compulsory allotment to what?

14th Oct – Got my third and last anti-dysentry injection today. Nip airforce quite active of late. Cat brought the kittens back to my bunk.

15th Oct – Evidently there is another move afoot as about 25 tradesmen (bricklayers etc) and three officers, Dowdall, Plunkett and Dr Beadnall have been confined to camp. I still have a feeling that we shall all be moved from here as the Nips have asked for return of people with longs and warm under-clothes and also rumours have come from the docks that all prisoners are to be shifted from Java. The local Gestapo have been quizzing the Aussis about their moves etc and have asked a lot of damn fool questions.

16th Oct – Well, it has come at last. It appears that all English troops are being moved to Japan and I am on the second party to go. Even the sick are going, tpt being provided for these and the Nips even ordered a dead man on to the party. Air raid siren went at 1030 but no results. Notices up along the road to Batavia warning the Wogs to beware of parachute troops; they appear to be getting the wind up.

17th Oct – Great bullshit parade today and I am 2nd i/c section 10 under Major Cutbush. Rumour has it that we leave tomorrow. Managed to buy a battle dress complete and sundry other things so am well prepared for the worst. Feel strangely calm about the whole move and still think that it may prove all for the best.

18th Oct – Still nothing definite as to when we shall pull out of here; managed to buy some bully and jam so now am pretty well stocked with provisions. It's a great pity I cannot take my 'koolie kittens', Big and Stinker, along with me as I get endless amusement out of watching their antics.

19th Oct – Parade today in our section. I am in No. 10. Started my packing. Every indication that we will NOT be going tomorrow but one can never tell with the Nips.

20th Oct – Paraded on the football pitch in the afternoon and had our kits searched by the Nips. Yesterday we were all given a green envelope with a piece of cellophane and had to give a sample stool for analysis. As these were dished out at 0830 and the completed article had to be returned by 0900 quite a lot of 'borrowing' went on. Think there is a chance that we may move tomorrow. Very good farewell concert at night.

And still Elizabeth and his folks back home had no idea of where he was or whether he was dead or alive. All of them remained in captivity.

British Prisoners of War Relatives' Association
PRISONER OF WAR AND CIVILIAN INTERNEE CAMPS
FAR EAST

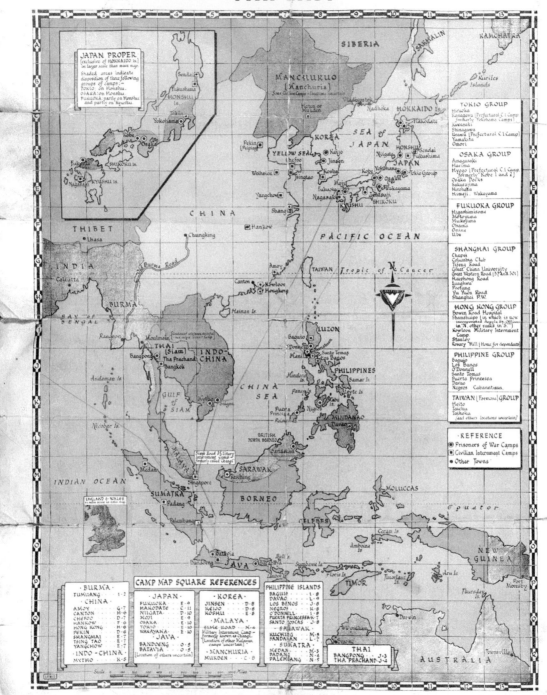

Revised up to January, 1945

PUBLISHED BY THE BRITISH PRISONERS OF WAR RELATIVES' ASSOCIATION
16a, ST. JAMES'S STREET, LONDON, S.W.1

PRICE 1/- ; By post 1/2

Chapter 6

They Were Transported Thus . . .

Both the diary and his narrative *Java, Jeopardy and Jail* paint a vivid picture of what happened over the next five weeks. The diary entries of the voyage north were necessarily brief but once incarcerated in Japan he expanded on these notes and included the account of the sea voyage as part of the book. This chapter is written using both accounts in their entirety, the diary entries (in italics) being dated accordingly and interspersed with narrative extracts. I leave him to relate this story.

Prisoners were transported thus . . . drawn by an American naval officer, Gus Johnson, after the nightmare voyage to Japan. The picture belies the hellish conditions the men had to endure below decks.

October–November 1942

"PRISONERS WERE TRANSPORTED THUS "

21st Oct   Left Uniekampong at 11. Went down to docks in a lorry and boarded the 'Yashida Maru' about 430. In all 2,000 POW on board accommodated in four holds and as the ship is about 5-6,000 tons the crush was terrific. Destination supposed to be Singapore where we change ships and then go on to Japan.

'The day before we left Uniekampong, the whole party was paraded on the football ground for a kit inspection which was carried out in a very perfunctory manner, my belongings - such as they were - never being looked at; people who had had cameras taken into custody by the Japs had those returned minus the film, and then we were given the order to dismiss for the day and parade again on the morrow at 11am with all our kit. I would point out at this stage that the Japs had detailed the numbers of those who were to leave and had made no effort to discriminate between the sick and the fit, and indeed, had managed to detail two people who were dead; when our own head-quarters pointed out this fact to them and asked to substitute fit personnel for the sick, the reply was, "Transport will be provided for those unfit to march down to the docks, the remainder will march carrying all they want to take with them whilst officers will be allowed one case or valise extra".

On the following day, being one of the sick, I was taken down to the docks on a lorry and dumped on the quayside to await the arrival of the main party which marched in about two hours later looking very hot and dusty having completed the three miles without a halt in the blazing heat of a tropical noon. In addition to the people from our camp, there was also a further party of over eight hundred mixed army and RAF from Batavia jail and Semplak aerodrome near Buiten-zorg bringing the total to over nineteen hundred. For the remainder of the day up till five o'clock in the evening we were kept on the dockside close to the ship which was being loaded with provisions and Dutch armoured cars - the latter being very effectively sabotaged within the next few days - neither food nor water being provided. Immediately prior to our embarking, the Japs went through all our heavy baggage removing camp beds and stools saying that these would not be needed as there were plenty of beds in Japan and mats were provided on the boat.'

22nd Oct   Sailed at 0900. Weather calm. Frank Knight also on board. Looks very fit.

'The ship which was taking us as far as Singapore was a dirty old cargo boat of some five thousand tons called the *Yashida Maru* and had four holds, two forward and two aft into which the nineteen hundred prisoners were crammed. Each hold was divided into two decks and on each deck, two wooden platforms, one 9" and the other 4' from the floor had been erected, the planking of these being covered with very thin rush matting which constituted our beds.

As can be guessed the heat inside the holds, both day and night was terrific and as we did not have sufficient room to lie down, we all felt pretty miserable at first, but cheered up when bread was issued at the rate of two loaves per head late at night. Nor was the sanitary question in any way better as there were three crude wooden latrines aft for the two holds there and six forward, the outlet from those being led over the side of the ship, whilst for ablutions we had two tanks of fresh water, the hospital accommodation being precisely nil. In the morning the decks were crammed solid with humanity trying to find a small corner to place a wash basin and often as not those who came last found that there was no more water left, and had to wait till the next day before they could obtain a wash. The meals were drawn in rusty iron buckets from the 'cookhouse' on the aft port side of the boat and were issued to us down in the holds where we queued up, and having received our portion of maggoty rice and stew containing the 'left overs' from the Japs' meal, retired onto our shelf to consume this awful stodgy mass at leisure.'

25th Oct   *Arrived at Singapore and lay at anchor outside.*

'We sailed the day after embarking and arrived off Keppel harbour Singapore four days later having taken a very roundabout course well outside the Banka Straits – probably due to this being unsafe for navigation, as a very large number of ships had been sunk there – and into Singapore from the East. Just outside the Horsbourgh light we ran into a Sumatra – a violent rainstorm accompanied by a high wind – so I went up on deck clad in my birthday suit armed with a tablet of soap and had a beautifully cool shower.'

26th Oct   *Moved into Keppel harbour. Docks showed very little signs of damage.*

'The following day we moved into Keppel and I was surprised at the small amount of damage that appeared to have been done as I was under the impression that the dock area had been subjected to very heavy bombing and shelling just prior to the fall, but apart from the sunken floating dock and a few demolished godowns, everything appear quite normal. There was also very little sign of damage on Puloh Bukum and Puloh Samboe where the big oil refineries and storage tanks were situated, but we did not pass very close to either of these islands so I cannot say much about them. There was also the remains of a crashed Hurricane fighter on Puloh Brani but this, too, seemed surprisingly intact.

We spent four days in Singapore and whilst there, managed to speak to some Australians who were imprisoned out at Changi, who said that they were being treated quite well and had received Red Cross supplies; they also mentioned that the Sikhs had gone over to the Japs but the Gurkhas were having a pretty thin time, having refused to sign any documents and had already killed six Sikhs and three Japs, the whole contingent being put on a rice and water diet for this.'

27th Oct   *Bath ashore and illegal operation performed.*

'During our second day at Singapore we were all taken ashore and told to strip on the quay, hoses then being turned on us. After the sweltering heat of the ship, this cold shower was magnificent but what followed was not so enjoyable as we were then paraded before six Japanese medical orderlies who told us to drop our pants and then thrust a glass rod up our backsides whilst a crowd of grinning coolies looked on. The object of this was to see if we had any carriers of dysentry amongst us and was the second 'test' which had been made within a week as, the day before we left Priok, each person had been issued with a piece of cellophane and envelope and ordered to produce a sample of stool within half and hour; as many were suffering from constipation and the Japs refused to wait a great deal of borrowing took place!!!'

28th Oct   *Col. Saunders party trans-shipped.*

'On the third day of our stay, the only occurrence of interest was the transhipping of eight hundred prisoners under Colonel Saunders . . .'

29th Oct   *Breakfast 0330 and spent day ashore being disinfested. Embarked at night on the 'Singapore Maru', 5,800 tons.*

30th Oct   *Sailed from Singapore.*

'. . . but on the fourth day, the remainder of us under Colonel Scott were given breakfast at 4am and disembarked with all our kit an hour later, spending the remainder of the morning sitting on the dockside beside a disinfecting ship while hordes of Nip troops were put through this, followed by a troupe of geisha girls, until finally our turn came, so having laid out all our gear on the concrete to be sprayed with disinfectant, we were led into the ship, which reminded me of something taken from a 'Fu Manchu' story complete with the noises of clanking machinery and peculiar odours, given a hot bath and cold shower while our clothes were being passed through an ammonia gas chamber and then we were dumped on the quayside to await the arrival of our next ship which, according to the Japs, was going to be much better with plenty of room, but which, in fact, proved to be even dirtier than our previous transport, but we did have room to lie down.

Once again we were accommodated in four holds with two tiers of platforms, the latrine position was the same as was that of ablutions and the officer who was lying next to me said very prophetically 'I'm afraid that many of us will not see the end of this journey' his words coming true in a few days when we had our first death five days later while lying at anchor off Cap St Jacques outside Saigon.

We had taken the disinfesting measures at Singapore to indicate that the ship we were boarding would be clean but soon discovered that bugs, cockroaches and a host of other undesirable animal life associated with filth swarmed in the holds while rats which in some cases were as big as cats came foraging for food amongst our baggage, and often as not, scurried over our recumbent forms at night. The geisha girls who we had seen at Singapore were also travelling on our ship and were accommodated in a small hold amidships, having to lie on similar mats to ours whilst some Jap officers occupied the few cabins that were available. The ship which was called the *Singapore Maru* was slightly larger than the *Yashida Maru* and was flush decked having an imitation ack, ack gun made of wood amidships, whilst a dummy depth charge apparatus with empty petrol drums representing the depth charges, was constructed in the stern; the actual armament of the vessel consisted of two small calibre guns one aft and the other right up in the prow which had every appearance of having been improvised from field guns.

After leaving Singapore, the sick roll steadily increased and it became clear that if some of the worst cases were not put ashore very soon, they would die, this matter being brought to the notice of the Japanese.'

Nov 3rd   *Arrived off Cap St Jacques outside Saigon. Spent the day at anchor. No sick taken ashore. Sailed again at 4pm for Formosa.*

'However, they refused to land anybody at Saigon, saying that there was no room in any of the hospitals, but gave us some iodine and bandages for the sick, sick who were suffering from dysentry! By the time we reached Formosa one officer and twenty men had died whilst about another two hundred were seriously ill, bacillary dysentry the chief complaint. One side of No. 3 hold had been taken over as a hospital and latrine buckets had been provided, but the accomodation was soon full up and men were lying on the floor of the hold under open hatches. Unfortunately, the officers' shelf was directly opposite the hospital and as we had to eat our meals on our beds, we looked straight on to this ghastly scene and could see men literally dying under our eyes and were completely helpless to do anything about it. As the number of sick increased, the medical staff found itself unable to cope with the numbers, and as some of the patients were too weak to stand and were unable to control themselves, they soiled their bedding and clothes and had to lie in the filth until some orderly could come along and try to clean it up. As the hold was swarming with flies and cockroaches which crawled over everything, it is a wonder that we did not have more casualties than we did.'

Nov 12th   *Arrived at Formosa (TaKao) 22 sick taken ashore on Nov 13th after we had asked for 200.*

'At Formosa, we again requested that two hundred of the more serious cases should be taken ashore, but the Japs would only permit twenty two to leave the ship, saying that there were no more beds available but that they would supply us with drugs and special food for the sick.

Nov 14th   *500 Nips came aboard and so we were more cramped than ever. Survivors of POW ship that was torpedoed in hospital ashore.*

'Just before we left Takao, an extra five hundred Jap troops were embarked, necessitating the removal of the hospital to the lower part of No. 3 hold, whilst the remaining 'fit' prisoners were crammed together so that, once again, it became impossible to lie full-length at night. During the last part of the voyage the weather became colder daily and with the increasing drop in temperature, there was a corresponding rise in the death roll as most of us had only tropical clothing and the sick had to combat cold as well as disease and also because the medical stores and food which we had been promised, did not materialise, our own meagre stock of medicines having been exhausted. Each morning there would be a number of bodies lying on the deck, wrapped up in blankets, awaiting burial and on the second last day, the number of deaths in one night reached the total of thirteen, whilst the padre who, himself, was suffering badly from the ravages of dysentery hardly had the strength to carry out the burial services.

Unfortunately, two of our four doctors became sick as well as most of the trained medical orderlies, so a request was made for volunteers which, unhappily, did not get a very good response as practically everybody on the ship was suffering from violent diahorrea and all day and night there was a long queue outside the latrines - which were only flushed out once each day – whilst conditions in the so-called hospital beggar description, the stench there being appalling as the only ventilation it had was one small hatchway about six foot square through which the wooden ladder led down to the deck of the hold, and as soon as somebody died, his corpse was carried onto the deck and a fresh patient took his place.

I have dealt at some length with the plight of the sick, but I feel that no words could convey the actual horror of the conditions and while there are a great many other points which I could write about regarding this topic, I shall not bore the reader by harping too much on the one subject.

The Jap troops who had come aboard at Formosa were not long in profiting by our miserable condition, as they raided their own store and bartered tins of M&V(meat and veg), Irish stew, and sugar for watches, wallets, fountain pens and any other small valuables which we possessed, driving very hard bargains. Unfortunately this 'changy-changy' practice led to a great deal of theft as the more unscrupulous element in our midst, having disposed of all their own belongings, did not hesitate to steal from their comrades both dead and alive, whilst the officers' baggage which was stacked in one of the holds was all thoroughly looted and in many cases, the only warm clothing that the officer possessed was taken and bartered.

The ships' food store was in No. 3 hold, the aft end of this hold being boarded off from the rest and a very large quantity of tinned meat, sugar, salt, cigarettes and sake was kept there. Each morning one of the Jap cooks would come down and draw the day's ration of sugar etc, one of our own men carrying this up to the cookhouse; it so happened that our shelf was very conveniently situated, for, when the sugar was being carried off, we frequently managed to scoop a large mugful hastily our of the bucket while the Jap's back was turned, our prize helping greatly put some flavour into our meals which consisted of rice - generally very old and dirty, – the leftover slops from the Jap's stew and tea which was tea in name only.

The stew was particularly nauseating as it was flavoured with radish and yeast extract and was probably responsible for a great deal of the stomach trouble as the radishes were very strong and our digestive system would not stand the strain imposed on it by these half raw vegetables after our starvation diet at Priok.'

Nov 15th   *Sailed in convoy but took shelter from storm that night. Food now very poor. No medicines for the sick on board despite Nip promises. Fruit overboard (Nov 23rd).*

'On the day that we left Takao in Formosa the sea was running very high and half a gale was blowing so, as the weather showed no signs of improving, we were forced to take shelter in the lee of one of the Pescadoes Islands, which lie to the west of Formosa. These islands are very bleak and barren and reminded me of the Shetlands, and on the island nearest to us we could quite plainly see a radio station and large aerodrome from which, from time to time, large twin-engined bombers would take off and head for the coast of China which lay only about a hundred miles to the West.

For four days we lay at anchor while the gale blew itself out and on the second day of our stay some Japs were playing cards under the open hatch of No. 2 hold when it started to rain. They then ordered one of our men to replace the hatch cover and when he indicated that he wanted an assistant to help him with the heavy planks, they kicked him on the shins and yelled, 'Hurry, hurry,' so the tommy departed up on deck while the players resumed their game. As he had anticipated, the hatch covers were far too heavy for him to lift unaided so he attempted to slide them into position; before he knew what was happening one of the boards slipped and plummetted down among the card players and laid one of them out with a fractured skull, which considerably cheered most of the prisoners who witnessed it.'

Nov 18th   *Sailed from anchorage which was close to very barren island with an aerodrome and wireless station. Up to today there has been 21 deaths mainly due to dysentry, and the Nips will do sweet FA to help the sick. CSM Jameson died yesterday from malaria. I have had one dose already on board and don't want another. Nips say that Russia has attacked them: perhaps: Food not too bad. Hope and believe condition will be better in Japan. Face slapped.*

Nov 25th   *Arrived off Moji in Japan. Lay at anchor and went alongside in the evening. 40 sick Americans from the PI (Philippine Islands) put on board. Since they gave in they have had 3,000 deaths mainly from dysentry. Store raided at night on a very large scale.*

'On the 25th of November we arrived off Moji Japan and lay at the quarantine anchorage for most of the day, having been five weeks en route from Java, moving alongside the wharf late in the afternoon, but despite all our requests that the sick be taken ashore, nothing was done in this respect, except that forty Americans from the Philippine

Islands were put on board our ship, all of them suffering from dysentry, and we were informed that we would disembark on the following morning. The Americans told us that they had received shocking treatment at the hands of the Japanese since they had surrendered and that three thousand out of seventeen thousand had died from dysentry and malaria, no medical supplies having been provided, and that when they were being marched to their prison camps, those who fell out due to sickness and disease were beaten over the head with a shovel and buried where they lay.

The weather was bitterly cold that night and as the Jap troops had been disembarked, the holds were much colder than usual, and I had just turned in for the night when there was an appalling row from the direction of the store and a few seconds later, one of our lads staggered past carrying a case of M&V disappearing into the lower hold. Very soon there was a regular procession to and from the storehouse which was emptied in record time, and we were treated to the spectacle of prisoners on a hell-ship reeling about in a state of helpless intoxication as a large quantity of sake – an alcoholic drink prepared from fermented rice – had been found and consumed on the spot. Having tired of watching their frolics, I was just dozing off to sleep again when I was rudely awakened by a sharp blow on the head and a very broad Scots voice saying, 'Here, sirrrr, here's some faags,' and there, lying beside me was a five hundred package of English cigarettes. Needless to say, I did not refuse these and Wing Commander Matthews who was next to me asked our benefactor if there was any sugar to be had, the reply to this being,

'Christ, Surr, there's f——ing tons o' it; here, gies a tin and ah'll get ye some,' and off he went into the store again. The same individual saw to it that the hospital was well supplied with food, cigarettes and sake and gave all the tins of condensed milk from the store to the doctors for distribution amongst the worst cases and I feel sure that more than one person owes his life to Bdr. O'Neil.

Realising that there was no hope of getting away from the boat without the raid being detected, I took immediate steps to conceal my ill-gotten gains and although officers were not searched on the following day, I'm pretty sure that, had they been, my share of the five hundred would not have been found.

Next morning there was the devil to pay! As soon as the robbery had been discovered, Nips prowled about the ship, stick in hand, looking for the culprits, even examining the cigarettes people were smoking, but meeting with no success, ordered that we return all that had been stolen. However, this was impossible, as the bulk of the food had been consumed during the night and when this was explained to them, they demanded that a list of names of those responsible was to be made and given to them so that they could be punished, but upon receiving a nominal roll of everybody left on the ship, announced that a search of kit and persons would be held, and if any stolen goods were found, the culprits would be shot and in any case, the officers would be punished as they must have known what was going on and should have taken steps to prevent it.

To my mind, this was just sheer nonsense as there were Jap guards sleeping in the hold who could not fail to have been wakened by the uproar, but as their own troops had been looting the store for days before our men entered it, they probably did not interfere so that they could save face and put the blame on our men.

In view of the robbery we were not disembarked in the morning and later in the day an English-speaking Jap came on board and proceeded to harangue the officers ending his remarks by saying, 'Are you civilised or are you savage?' In my opinion it would have been more appropriate if we had asked him that question considering the treatment we had received.'

Nov 26th   *Disembarked at 4pm. One lad committed suicide bring[ing] total of deaths up to 63. Went by barge to Ube. Quarters not too bad. Thank God that awful voyage is finished. Big shindy about raid on store. Was like sitting on top of a volcano the whole time. Most of the lads down with violent squitters. Our new guards seem much more reasonable.*

'We disembarked that evening leaving about 350 sick on board who were too ill to move and while assembling on the quayside, learned that yet another death had occurred as one of the soldiers had committed suicide, bring the total of deaths for the voyage to sixty three - just about double the number we had had during our seven months in Java. For four long hours, we were kept standing on the docks in an icy wind which cut through our thin tropical clothing while our baggage was examined by the Customs to see if we were bringing any dutiable goods into the country, and then went through the usual rigmarole of counting and recounting before being marched off in parties of one hundred and seventy, past the ship on which the Americans had travelled and seeing some of their sick lying on the concrete with no covering, to where barges were waiting to transport us to our respective camps in neighbouring mining villages on the coast of the Inland Sea.'

Chapter 7

Motoyama: Camp No. 8 Fukuoka District

November 1942–April 1943

Nov 28th–30th *Settling in period. One death in camp. I had to do the burial service. Sick myself with bad cough and squitters. Sharing a room with Morton, Kinnear and Maclean.*

This was a foretaste of what was to come. The camp was Motoyama (no. 8), one of a number which formed part of the Fukuoka administrative department covering the southern area of Honshu and the northern part of Kyushu (see back flap). It was described by the International Red Cross (IRC) delegate, Mr Paravacini, in his report dated 15 April 1943, as:

'. . . located at Motoyama, near Shimonoseki, sunny and healthy site, over-
looking the Inland Sea . . . comprising single storey wooden barracks,
formerly workmen's dormitory, spacious living quarters . . .'

Before long, Atholl had put his draughtsman's skills to good use by drawing a detailed plan of the camp in one of his notebooks (see next page).

The following extracts from the diary cover the period December 1942 to April 1943. During this time Atholl described in detail what the day-to-day existence was like, not just for the prisoners but also the Japanese. He observed the relationships between prisoners – OR's and officers, officers and senior officers – and these groups and the Japanese, often with humour. He talked about home and it is clear how important communicating with the family was for his sanity and self-preservation. It was the lead up to his first Christmas in Japan:

Dec 1st–5th *Two more deaths from dysentry. Have been issued with 'warm' clothing, blanket sheets and boots so now am not too badly off for clothing. Been down the mine once already and the effort nearly creased me: Food not too bad but not sufficiently sustaining.*

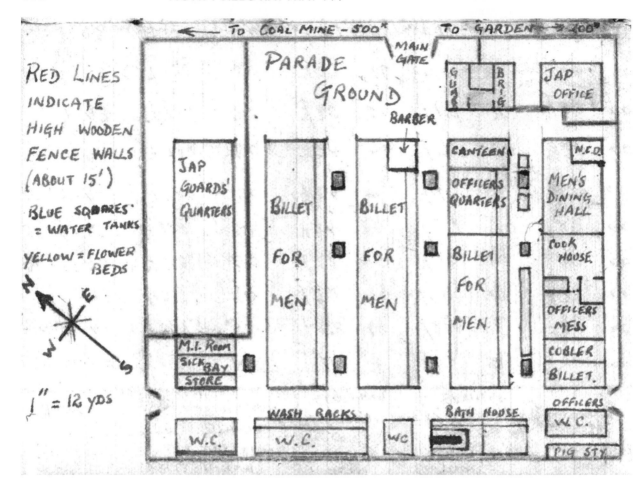

Diagram of Motoyama POW Camp, Japan.

Was slashed across the face while out on working party. Great deal of aerial activity. Have been feeling far from well, chest being none too bright, and long for the days when all this will be a thing of the past. Cigarette situation none too good and am reduced to smoking 'tabs' (these were specially rolled cigarettes: all the stubs from previous cigarettes were saved and when there were sufficient to make one whole one the stubs were wrapped in fine paper and smoked. They were so strong that he said they almost blew your head off!)

Dec 6th–7th   *Weather very cold now, the surrounding hills having been mantled with snow. Down the mine again on the 7th. Another death in the camp due to dysentry and malnutrition. Feeling bloody at night and think I am in for another bout of malaria. Nips issued us with 10 cigarettes. Nearly*

*everybody in camp has a bad cough and inflamed throat but all the Jap
doctor prescribes is MgSo4 and Bi (magnesium sulphate and bicarbonate).
Wonder when this business will be over; can't be too soon.*

Dec 8th–11th   *Two more deaths. Been issued with greatcoats and cowls.
Down the mine again which did not do my throat any good. Men supposed to
start work down the mine tomorrow. Weather very cold and unpleasant.
Today (11th) air-raid warning from 10 -12. No developments. Had an acute
bout of homesickness of late and wonder how everyone is getting on at home.*

Dec 12th   *Men down the mine today. Japs produced a newspaper in
English for us today but apart from very occasional snatches of real news, it
is mostly propaganda. It appears that we have invaded Tunisia and Lybia
offensive has started; also Darlan has come over to us. Throat still very sore
and cough none too good. Much aerial activity and MG practice.*

Dec 13th–16th   *It now seems evident that officers are not going to be forced
to do down the mine for we have not gone down since the 12th. Food has
improved immensely and I now feel quite well fed. Col. Petrie has done very
well with the Japs and although some people criticise, I have no complaints
whatsoever. Wonder if we shall still be here this time next year. Cigarettes
question tends to be serious at times. Went for walk on 16th and enjoyed it
very much.*

Dec 17th   *Down with another bout of malaria but it is not too severe. Some
days I just can't be bothered making any entries in the diary and I find that
time is inclined to pass very slowly. We all miss the T.S.F. as it appears from
the paper we get, that quite a lot of very interesting and significant events
have taken place since we left Priok. Nips issued us with two more blankets
and asked us what we would like for Xmas. On the whole, conditions have
improved since we came to Japan and I don't think they should deteriorate.
Wish the Japs would get a move on and pay us as we have three months pay
due to us.*

Dec 18th   *Sixth death occurred two days ago and I think that the Nips are
feeling a bit concerned about our mounting death roll. One officer per day to
go down the mine with the men. Why? And also why are the field officers not
on the roster for the mine? Nips being quite liberal with cigarettes these days.*

Dec 19th   *The men are not being worked too hard down the mine as the
conveyor belt is constantly stopping; we have a few miners in our crowd and
they have been able to 'instruct' the men on a good few points! From what we
can glean from the newspaper, things seem to be going quite favourably for the
Allies and I have noted that no mention is made of the Solomon area.*

Dec 20th   *Got an issue of oranges today which proved a very welcome treat.
The Jap doctor was told yesterday that I had malaria but did not come and*

see me; today he sent me some epsom salt powders with instructions that they were to be taken 5 times daily!!! I wish that one of our own doctors would appear on the scene for this fellow is an absolute quack ...I had a very vivid dream of home last night which has set me wondering how they all are getting on. Oh, when is this bloody war going to end?

Dec 21st   *A very quiet day on the whole. A ban has been laid on any further buying in the village. Still on quinine course and have been feeling far from well, as I still have my cough and have developed a cold as well... and when the hell are the Nips going to pay us, as we now have 3 months due. Another death in camp bringing the total to 8 or 5% of our strength in 4 weeks. Great deal of aerial activity after dark. Have not had a smoke for three days now but this has not worried me unduly. Am feeling very browned off with the world in general and my own predicament in particular. When ARE we going to be free again?*

Dec 22nd   *Every day is the same here, just a case of getting up to eat and then retiring under the blankets again for we have no fires in the rooms – no charcoal issue for well over a week now – and it is bitterly cold; more often than not the meals are not worth going for as supper is the only one that could in any way be called substantial. When mother used to tell me, 'someday you'll wish you could get this ...', I never thought that these words were going to prove true. However, I have saved a tin of bully and a tin of M&V (meat and veg) for our Xmas dinner so we shall have a little treat then.*

Dec 23rd   *Got up for supper last night but did not feel too clever. Kinnear on night-shift down the mine so he's not feeling any too pleased with life. Our Dutch money has been changed by the Nips at the rate of f1,00 = Y1.00 or just about half the true rate. Well, I guess that this will prove the bluest Xmas I have had as there is next to nothing to eat, absolutely nothing to smoke either in the camp or village, nowhere to go and worst of all nobody to see. What wouldn't I do to get out of this lot! Weather still bitterly cold and still no fires. In fact, the whole bloody outlook stinks!!*

Dec 24th   *The Japs have promised us quite a few things for our Xmas and much to our surprise and delight kept their word. In the evening, the mine manager provided a gramophone and a good selection of records, Jazz and serious to which we listened after supper when an issue of cigarettes and wine was made. When selections from Mozart and Beethoven were being played my thoughts went to home and I wondered how soon it would be before our re-union. All the Nips very affable during the concert and, in fact, we spent a most enjoyable evening.*

Dec 25th   *The food today has been marvellous! For breakfast we had barley porridge and sugar – we followed this up with bully sandwiches and cocoa in the forenoon – for lunch pork, boiled spuds, cabbage and spaghetti whilst for supper, beef stew, roast spuds, beans, cabbage, duff with sugar sauce, and*

Example of Japanese money.

bread biscuits butter and wine. In the afternoon we were inspected by a Nip major and later had to move to our new quarters and, of course, I had to be orderly officer. In all, we had a far better Xmas than we ever dared hope for and I do feel the Japs did their best to give us a good time. A sing-song concert at night round the fire in the men's dining hall rounded off the best day of our captivity so far.

Dec 26th   *Very busy all day getting the new quarters into shape. Japanese carpenters who were working in the billet have been very friendly, buying cigarettes and foodstuffs for us and smuggling them in past the guard – no extra being charged. Big rumpus at night over the mines question, skin and hair flying freely on occasion. Had a return of the squitters probably due to the Xmas feed. Very cold at night, snow and sleet with high wind. News seems very good as the Russians are evidently going strong and our east and west pushes in N. Africa seem to be meeting with success; as far as we can make out, Rommel has been driven out of Lybia into Tripolitania, and is not too confident about holding that.*

Dec 27th   *Definitely brass monkey weather these days! Have not been feeling too well as my eyes are giving trouble and my bowels and stomach ditto. Kinnear spent the morning making a card table and just when it was completed, the sentry came in and smashed it for firewood. Morton down the mine last night and says it was foul; I am down on the roster to go tomorrow morning and when I approached the Col. to try and get my turn postponed in view of my recent attack of malaria, he refused to have anything to do with it and, needless to say when I asked some of the others to change places with me all had some excuse for not doing it. All I hope is that I do not do any damage to my heart as it is pretty tough going up and down that filthy sewer. Not been sleeping too well of late, probably due to the cold.*

Dec 28th   *Up at 5am for the mine today, and was it cold! When we reached the coal face, I was parked in an out of the way corner for seven long hours but fortunately I had taken a book down with me so the time did not lag too much. Gardening for the officers started today and from all the reports is not too strenuous or unpleasant. Managed to persuade the Nip commandant to buy 100 cigarettes for me so now have a smoke for the next three days or so. Felt absolutely creased by the time I got back to camp. Troops feeling very discontented with the rations they are getting and certainly they are not sufficiently sustaining for the work that they have to do.*

Dec 29th   *Feeling bloody awful today. Did a big washing in the morning but had to retire to bed in the afternoon only to wake up with a violent dose of squitters. As the Nips celebrate New Year instead of Xmas, five days holiday has been declared from the 31st–4th inclusive and the labour manager has promised us bread, butter and sake as well as music for a New Year treat. It would be much more to the point if he gave us some decent food for this rice and cabbage stew is not doing us any good and is quite inadequate to keep out the cold. Newspapers rather interesting today as details of their naval losses are given and they admit losing quite a fair amount. A great deal of prominence is being given to the assassination of Darlan, one day they blame Roosevelt and next Churchill. They also appear to be getting uneasy about the war in Europe and certainly are far from happy about the state of affairs in the SW Pacific. Roll on the day when we sail from this damned country, and get back to civilisation.*

Dec 30th   *Stayed in bed most of the day as my tummy is all out of order and the prospect of wielding a spade in the garden did not appeal to me. Food ration very poor these days, hardly enough to even temporarily satisfy the hunger that the cold gives us, and from what Trillwood says, we can expect even less in the future. Morton comes out with some very amusing expressions on occasion, today he described that giggling bitch who accompanies the doctors as having 'teeth like tombstones' – a very apt summary of her smile. Have been having a series of very vivid dreams about the folks at home of late and am feeling rather disturbed about this as they are bound to be worried about my welfare even if they do know that I am a POW and heaven only knows they have enough worries as it is without having that additional one. Col. Petrie had another chat with the mine manager and managed to convince him of the futility of officers going down the mine so we are to go gardening instead – which is a good thing. Also the Nips said that we should be able to write home in the near future and if they keep their word that is a very big step in the right direction.*

Dec 31st   Everything very quiet today. Stayed in bed as my squitters had not improved. In the afternoon, the Japs started playing gramophone records and they had quite a good selection ranging from 'Lady of Spain' to 'Ave Maria'. In the evening quite a lot of fish, apples and oranges arrived but unfortunately most of the fish and oranges were rotten so the expected "big eats" did not materialise. There was also an issue of sake and biscuits but the one thing that we really wanted i.e. cigarettes, failed to appear and the men were rather disgusted.

Stayed up to see in the New Year, the last person I saw in 1942 and the first I saw in 1943 was Elizabeth as I looked at her photo during the change. Well, 1942 has been the most disastrous year in my sweet young life and I can only hope that the New Year will see the return of peace to this war-weary world, and that we can return to all those so near and dear to us, and find them safe and well. As Mac said, we are going to find a great many big changes when we get out of here for all our friends have been scattered to the four winds and our loved ones are bound to have changed with the passage of time.

It was just as well that he didn't know he would spend a further two Christmases as a prisoner of war. For now, he was learning to find his way through each day, keeping up with his diary entries and trying hard not to think about the future. This task had become a little easier as the commandant at Motoyama when they arrived was not so strict about prisoners keeping journals, sometimes even supplying them with paper and notebooks. It had been a different story in Tandjong Priok where it had been a very hazardous occupation and he had had to keep his diary writing to a minimum, making brief entries, often in code, in a small pocket book (see p. 63). Some of the prisoners of war, officers as well as men, were very indiscreet in the early days and this led to problems for everyone.

In this more relaxed atmosphere he began to develop the idea for his and Des Campion's book *Java, Jeopardy & Jail.* He started to document their trials and tribulations while on the run in Java. In the finished book, chapter 6 begins with the following observation,

As the reader will appreciate, in a prison camp it is of vital importance to keep one's mind off the past, and future, and just live from day to day, having some form of mental and physical outlet, for once a person indulges in self-pity or sinks too deep into depression, he becomes a physical and mental wreck with no willpower or spirit to combat illness when it comes, and is an encumbrance to his fellow men who have enough troubles of their own without having to listen to those of one who will do nothing towards helping himself.

And so, by the end of 1942 he had sampled work down the mines for the first time (and it certainly wouldn't be the last) and he had weathered repeated attacks of malaria and the bitter cold, neither of which would go away for long. Bouts of homesickness still overwhelmed him but all in all he was coping, somehow. The diary entries continue . . .

1943

Jan 1st–12th   *I had meant to keep a daily diary starting from the New Year, but today (12th) was the first opportunity I had of committing anything to paper due to the lack of this commodity.*

The Nips have been put into a tremendous flap as a General – i/c POW – is coming to inspect our camp on the 16th and, as usual, have been issuing orders right, left and centre, then countermanding the whole issue. The newspaper we get 'The Nippon Times' has been making a great fuss over Nanking China's entry into the war, but, of late, has been very quiet about the fighting in Europe and the SW Pacific, and has made only passing reference to the fighting in Burma which, to my mind is rather significant.

Turning to affairs more immediately concerning us, the garden is coming on very nicely, large quantities of onions, beans and cabbage having been planted, and when the weather is fine, it is grand to go out there and spend a morning in the sunshine, working only when we feel inclined stopping to watch the MG practice of the young 'Wild Eagles' and shipping on the Inland Sea. At first the sentries who came out with us, started to 'Kora' and shout whenever we broke off digging for a smoke or rest, but we soon let them under-stand that we were NOT on fatigues, and what we did – or rather – what we did not do was no concern of theirs ...The food question is far from satisfac-tory as we get no bread issue from the Japs and have no flour to bake our own; the supply of cooking oil has run out and has not been replaced whilst fresh fish is just a memory.

Jan 13th–14th   *Mother's birthday today; I wonder how they are all getting on back in old St Andrews. The weather has suddenly turned very cold and a heavy fall of snow, followed by hard frost played havoc with the water system in camp as the mains burst and we had no water for bathing, laundry etc. whilst the cookhouse has been severely rationed. The Col. decided that, as the rooms had been plastered, no fires were to be lit in the billets until the fire-places were completed but, having frozen for one day we all said, 'To hell with this' and proceeded to light roaring furnaces to dispel the chill.*

Jan 15th–16th   *I'm bloody fed up! Our rations have been cut down again, the weather is damned cold and I WOULD have to be orderly officer on the day that that old fool, the Nip General came to inspect our quarters. We were*

all paraded on the 'square' to salute him when he arrived and had to stand about in an icy wind for half an hour before he came. He spoke very little English and asked the Col. if he could speak German which he couldn't; the men were very bolshie all day with regard to fatigues and there was a grand uproar in the dining hall at night over the rations given to the late shift of miners. The Jap RSM Okamoto, has given out that we shall be able to send a postcard to the folks at home in the near future but our powers that be have made no attempt to press the matter and when questioned about progress about this as well as pay for the officers, hum and haw and never give a satisfactory answer.

The Col. told a Japanese Col. i/c POW in this area that we are very comfortable here and are "quite happy"!!!! – and made no attempt to ask for the hundred and one things we really need. Of course, he's all right in his new office with a proper stove to keep it warm, so the old FYJ policy is in operation again. Oh, damn this bloody war.

Promises about writing home would be made and broken many times before any communication was finally established. During the next few months the act of writing a letter or card took on a huge significance. Even though it was frustrating for them, Atholl and his fellow prisoners were lucky (at Motoyama and later on at Zentsuji) as many allied prisoners never got word to their families or received any letters during the whole time they were captive. In the event, his collection contains no fewer than 49 letters, cards and even a telegram sent to him while he was in camp.

Jan 17th   I forgot to mention in my entry for the 13th that the men had suffered their first casualty down the mine, a L/Cpl. having been caught by a fall of coal and had his leg broken in three places. So far as I know there has been no effort made to tap the Nips about compensation. Have not spent a very pleasant day as I just about froze last night and was unable to get the 'steam up' all day . . . Our photos were taken about a week ago for identification purposes, each officer receiving a copy of his own particular effort. As usual, mine turned out to be pretty ghastly and F/Lt. Hutcheson (late 100 squadron RAF) remarked on seeing it, 'You seem to have got 5 years hard without the option,' which just about filled the bill.

I wonder how all the folks at home are getting on and whether they have received any notification of my still being alive – if not at large. Well, that must be all for tonight as it is now bath time and I hope to get warm for the first time today.

Original ID photographs taken at Motoyama, January 1943.
Atholl wrote on the back of his photograph.

Contrary to Atholl's hopes, there was still no news of his whereabouts and back home life was very challenging. Elizabeth had started her house surgeon's job at St Luke's and was kept very busy from the start with little time off to rest. His father continued his quest for information and about this time wrote again to the War Office seeking any further news.

Jan 18th   *Had quite a busy day as we made some structural alterations to the billet, my contribution being an extension to the electric light to our new 'drawing room' – funnily enough, it worked. Mac has got a deal under way for his watch, 40 yen being his lowest figure, so if this comes off we should be able to keep the wolf from the door for a short while at least. A small party went into Ube today to see an oculist and from all the reports they brought back it is not the imposing city it appears to be when viewed from our village (Motoyama) across the bay for, apart from a modern cinema and a very few modern shops and sundry factories reputed to be manufacturing cement, the whole place is made up from wooden shacks similar to those in which we live; unfortunately our party could buy neither food, clothing nor tobacco as all these were strictly rationed. I have noticed that our room is the only place in camp where laughter is heard, the other messes being rather gloomy affairs; much of our amusement is derived from stories told by the various occupants, Morton in particular having a very good fund of yarns about his seafaring experiences, whilst Mac comes out with a really drole joke every now and then. Most of our topics of conversation would be barred by any literary and debating society, the natural daily functions of the body coming well to the fore . . .*

Jan 19th   *Went out gardening in the morning as I felt more energetic than usual and spent the morning swinging a truncle in fine style; on returning to camp I set to work sawing up some logs with great gusto. After lunch I felt very shivery and out of sorts so, recognising the symptoms, got my temperature taken, found it to be 102° in the shade, gobbled down a dose of quinine and retired to bed with yet another bout of malaria.*

Jan 20th   *Much about the same today. Weather very cold and it is utterly miserable lying on the floor in this beastly room feeling the cold gradually eating into one, inspite of a hot water bottle improvised out of a Dutch water bottle, having nothing to read, no one to talk to, for everyone goes out to get the steam up, and very little to eat. As I lay in bed, I gave the old memory a good spring clean and envisaged all the good times I had enjoyed before and during this war, caravan holidays, games of golf, walks and dances with Elizabeth, evenings with the old folks, fishing trips, 'rags' at University, flying at Singapore and a host of others. The only trouble with this form of mental escape is that sooner or later you must come back to earth, the jolt of this being pretty terrific.*

Jan 21st   Feeling much better today but still am pretty groggy. Dreamed last night that the war was over and that I was back home with the folks again . . . The troops make a habit of going sick with coughs and colds as often as possible, the reason for this being that they have discovered that the cough mixture prescribed by the doctor goes very well with the rice.

Jan 22nd   Feeling better today but as I am still taking quinine stayed in bed; weather very unpleasant as it is very raw and cold. Opinion as to how long we will be incarcerated differs greatly, some believing we shall be free by Xmas, others, including myself, think that next summer should see the end of it all, whilst a few pessimists (I hope) are steeling themselves for a three year spell in 'durance vile' . . . Rumour has it that our guards are going to be changed tomorrow, this being quite likely as it was the custom in Java to change them about every two months, their new destination being Shonan, or as we know it, Singapore. There are supposed to be four POW camps in the immediate vicinity of Motoyama and I expect that their occupants are the remnants of our party. Oh, for a really good square meal of English food!!!

His information regarding other camps was correct as according to the International Red Cross report made in April 1943, there were four camps in the area: Ube, Motoyama, Ohama and Higashi Misome near Shimonoseki, and they did indeed contain the rest of the British prisoners from Java who were shipped on the *Singapore Maru*. There were 16–18 officers and roughly 100 OR's held in each camp and there was little or no contact between them.

Jan 23rd   We got big news late last night as the Jap RSM told the Col. that Red Cross parcels would be arriving for us today; naturally, there has been a great deal of speculation as to what they will contain and I am hoping for some food and woollen goods. One of the more amusing aspects of this life is the behaviour of individuals when reveille is sounded. Morton is generally up first and when he is dressed, he gives Mac a call, who heaves a sigh and then leaps out of bed like a scalded cat and flings on his clothes, interspersing shivers with such phrases as 'Oh shit, it's cold', which utterances in no way encourage others to follow his spartan example. When roll call is sounded half an hour later, most of us have managed to crawl blasphemously out of bed, but Kinnear has managed to time his rising to a nicety, dressing in a welter of arms and legs, appearing on parade just in time to salute and be reported present.

Jan 24th   *The Red Cross supplies arrived yesterday and were portioned out amongst us all; as only fifteen parcels came for the whole camp, each article was balloted, my luck running to a small tin of meat galantine; Mac receiving a beef steak pudding. In addition to these tinned goods were cocoa and sugar in bulk, a share in these being about 1¼ lbs of the latter and about 2 ozs of the former. As the Nips made an issue of a shirt and long drawers, we have had quite a gala day. Mac and I have pooled our stores — the galantine has been consumed already — and it is funny (peculiar, not ha ha) to think that things which seemed to constitute the bare necessities of life such as butter, bread, and meat in any form have now become super luxuries, and it is a great day in our drab and dreary lives when we get an issue of any one of these. Perhaps I have a suspicious nature, but I did think it odd that there were no cigarettes or woollen goods in the parcels!*

Jan 25th–28th   *Have more or less got over my last bout of fever but have managed to collect a filthy cold — small wonder when people persist in coughing and sneezing open-mouthed, to say nothing about drying unwashed handkerchiefs over the fire . . .*

Jan 29th–30th   *For no apparent reason, the Japs, from the RSM down to the lowliest sentry, have suddenly turned very sour towards us . . .*

Jan 31st   *Very cold today with intermittent snow. The 'Motoyama POW Horticulture Society' held a general meeting in the officers' mess after breakfast to decide about a roster for the morning and afternoon parades to the garden: much to my relief Mac and I were drawn for the same party, this being very convenient as we go 50-50 with any cigarettes we get . . . At the present moment, I am seated in the men's dining hall, it is after 'lights out' but the two Japs who are playing table tennis are quite content to let me stay. There is a roaring log fire in the stove and as I have just had a hot bath, followed by a cup of cocoa and a pipe of tobacco, I am feeling more or less at peace with the world and just in the frame of mind when memories and visions of home slowly drift though my mind and the unpleasant realities of the present sink into temporary oblivion.*

The picture this conjures up reminds me so vividly of Dad during his last weeks. Wearing pyjamas and a thick woolly dressing gown, he sat beside a roaring log fire in his armchair in the bed-sitting room we had made for him in the lounge. Not content with a warm glow he had to keep stoking the fire so that it burned like a furnace, making the room feel sub-tropical. I don't suppose he ever forgot just how cold he had once been.

Feb 1st   At long last, the postcards which we are to be allowed to send home have arrived and apart from the usual security precautions on both sides, we're not restricted in what we may say. Officers are to be permitted to write a PC or letter once a week, OR's restricted to the same once a fortnight. We had a bit of bad news in that the RSM has received his marching orders and will be leaving us in the near future; apparently, he is not being replaced, but as he has done a lot towards making our life here as 'pleasant' as it is, he is about the only Jap I have met who could be called anything approaching a gentleman, for he does show a great deal of consideration in his dealings with us. Our cubby hole is much envied by one and all, especially in the cold evenings, as the whole seven of us, Mac, Morton, Kinnear, Whitty, Campbell, Webber and self all gather round a blazing log fire arguing and yarning to our hearts' content – occasionally having a hate session against some new decree or some person in the mess.

More original ID photographs taken at Motoyama, January 1943.

Major Campbell

Feb 2nd . . . For the past few days, I have had a desire to continue with the book that Campion and self started in Java, but somehow or other, I cannot get into the proper reminiscent state of mind for this, except at night, just after the bath and cup of cocoa, but then we have to go to bed so the job never gets done. However, one of these days I'll really get down to it and bring it right up to date. The troops have been very bolshie of late, even going so far as to tell that slimy swine, Ono, that 'the Col. is a f—ing old bastard who starves them (the miners) to feed himself' and whenever they decide that their ration is insufficient they show it to him and say, 'that's all that they have given us at camp –' although they get an extra meal a day and all the 'perks' and have already eaten a good portion of the food supplied for the boxes. At first, I had a good deal of sympathy for them, but now I have only disgust. In some cases, too, their sanitary habits have degenerated into those of an untrained dog, for, rather than walk a matter of 15–20 yds to the latrines during the night, some of them ease their bowels and bladders in the passages inside the blocks.

Feb 3rd–5th   Of late, I have been having very vivid dreams which take the form of life after this war is over and, funnily enough, Bill features in them quite a lot; poor devil, he has been a prisoner in Germany for three years now and must be getting pretty fed up with it. [Bill Moore was a friend and fellow St Andrews student who was taken prisoner at Dunkirk – see photo, page 22, Chapter 2.]

The newspapers have intensified their 'hate campaign' against the Americans in particular, hardly a day passing without some reference being made to alleged acts of brutality committed by the 'dough boys' in the southern fronts, in some cases, the leading article being devoted to this; such words as 'beastiality', 'devils in human guise' etc. are in common use . . .

Feb 6th   Orderly dog again today . . . I have been feeling very much more optimistic as a result of the news as well as feeling reasonably healthy and fit; my first postcard to the folks at home was posted today and although it will probably be months before they get it and can reply, I feel as though contact with them had been re-established and somehow they seem to be much nearer and I can look forward to seeing them all again. In short, my morale has gone up by leaps and bounds. I thoroughly enjoy writing up this diary and fear that, on occasion, I become rather long-winded but believe – pardon my conceit – that it should make quite interesting reading at some future date.

Feb 7th   Spent the morning in the garden and had to work hard as there was a biting wind coming from the North; however, once I got the steam up, it was quite pleasant. Yesterday, I was on a court of inquiry to investigate responsibility for an accident which happened to one of our troops when he was working down the mine. A lump of the roof fell on him and injured his back and from the evidence it appears that the Nips are forcing the pace down the mine to such an extent that timbering cannot keep abreast of the work. When we were required to go down I was always in a blue funk as in many places large areas looked very unsafe, and falls were frequent, and I had a horror of being trapped down there by a major fall. I might as well give a resume of a day in the life of a POW: Reveille, 0730, roll call, 0800, breakfast of rice and 'relishes'?, 0830, gardening 1000–1200, lunch (rice and 'stew'?) 1245, supper, (rice, stew or fish, occasionally meat (1oz)) 1830, lights out 2130. Yesterday, the Nips suddenly produced some forms which the men were required to fill in, and stated that we (the officers) were not to coach the men in the answers; having read the questions which were of a very leading nature, steps were taken to see that nothing which would be of use for propaganda would be put down and although I did not see the completed forms, I heard that they were quite useless to the Nips, many having taken the opportunity to have sly pokes at our captors. One question was 'Whom do you love, adore or worship?' this being answered by some as 'Winston Churchill' whilst somebody put 'King George VI, His Britannic Majesty, Emperor of India, and Defender of the Faith'.

Feb 8th–10th   . . . Bombardier Young whilst working down the pit, was being chivvied by some little upstart of a Nip so he told him to get out of his way; this the Nip refused to do, so Young promptly crowned him with a shovel!! and was only warned 'not to be so rough' when brought up before the Nip camp commandant for it. I have discovered that the only way to get anything out of these Nips is to be as bold as brass and ask for twice what you want. In this respect, we ran out of cigarettes so I went to the guard to get permission to go out and buy some in the village but was referred to the office. There I asked for 100 fags for four officers and they must have misunderstood me for I got 200 fags!!!

Feb 11th   Now that we have some money, an attempt is being made to buy some books, and I have requested information regarding textbooks in Chemistry, Physics and Maths so that I shall not lose touch altogether with these subjects. A great deal of discussion takes place in our cubby-hole at night as to whether the Japs will fight on after the collapse of Germany when she will be faced with the armed might of Britain, USA and very probably Russia as well. Kinnear, who has been in Japan prior to this war, thinks that they will fight to the bitter end, but I have a feeling that they already see the writing on the wall and will be only too glad to get peace . . .

Feb 12th   The Nips put a fast one over us today as when we were seated at breakfast, word came via the orderly officer that eight officers and twenty men were required for road fatigue and that there would be no gardening today. After some debate, we went out with the party and found that we were expected to stack pit props at the mine head; this we refused to do and came to a compromise with the guard, pushing two handcarts loaded with wood back to the camp . . . After lunch, they called for us again so we went en bloc to the office and lodged a strong protest which elicited the information that Ono was at the back of it all. The Nip inspector general of coalmines was paying a visit today and I expect he wanted to show us off – or perhaps up. After very little argument we went gardening instead; that man Ono is one person I should like to have for ten minutes when we are freed from here. Another 'irregularity' that was noted today was the fact that an empty carton which had once held Red Cross supplies appeared on the rubbish dump, a Jap having been seen placing it there. Many of the officers and men have come out in a very irritating rash, the crotch and elbows, stomach and legs being the chief areas of infection. Many reasons for this have been put forward, but I am of the opinion that it is due to a vitamin deficiency as we are now getting very little in the way of fresh vegetables.

Major R. J. S. Earle, RA. Motoyama, January 1943.

Feb 13th 1,500 grapefruit were brought into camp today with the injunction that they were to be issued at the scale of one per head until they were finished.

The Japs had a heyday detailing people for the mine and wanted to send down almost every man in the camp including cookhouse staff and sanitary men but Major Earle managed to get this readjusted. Sgt. Cassidy got into trouble with the guard and had his face slapped for bringing the mining shift from the pithead to camp, stopping en route for cigarettes without waiting for an escort.

Feb 14th–16th Orderly dog again today: this seems to be coming round too frequently these days, the RAF having two sick in their number; however, now that the Japs have completely taken over the administration of the camp, the duties are not very arduous.

Feb 17th . . . Now that the Nips are clamping down on people for the mine, the men are beginning to realise that Ono and his satellites are not their fairy godfathers and are becoming more 'British minded', as opposed to 'bolshie' . . .

Feb 18th–21st Today, being a holiday, the Japs decided to hold a kit inspection and, as usual, made a complete bog up of it, getting thoroughly bad tempered in the course of it all. I made rather a bloomer by laughing outright in their faces which, naturally, did not improve matters . . . We got word of the neighbouring POW camp and they appear to have had 19 deaths, including W/Cdr. Frow, Sq./Ldr. Barnley, and 2/Lt. Hunt who passed on with pneumonia and we have been told that our camp with its eight deaths has the lowest death rate of any of those who arrived with us. The people from

*the other camp spoke highly of their treatment and said that they were quite
pleased with their living conditions, and had received the same number of Red
Cross parcels as us. I found that letter writing was extremely difficult as there
is so much I want to tell the folks at home and yet, due to censorship regs so
little that one can say; however, I am going to write my letters day by day from
now onwards and may be able to overcome this difficulty by doing that . . .
Food none too good of late.*

Feb 22nd *The news has been very good of late and it is apparent from the
tone of articles in the 'Nippon Times' that Germany is being pretty hard
pressed in Russia . . .*

Feb 23rd–26th *Not a great deal to relate over this period . . . Today (26th)
we went for a long ramble round the promontory and then scaled the high hill
at the back of the village, and were rewarded with a most gorgeous view for
our trouble, as the visibility was exceptionally good and the weather perfect;
the panorama which stretched out below us was very similar to the view from
the top of Table Mountain looking out over the bay. Felt very pleasantly
fatigued by the time we got back to camp and would like to do that walk every
day. Distance covered was between 5 and 6 miles. Wrote to the folks at night.*

Feb 27th *Went for another ramble round the coast today and thoroughly
enjoyed it as the weather was beautifully warm. The little Jap corporal who
acts as our escort seems to look forward to these perambulations about as
much as we do and tries very hard to be amiable, and always stops going
through the village to let us buy cigarettes. One of the few pleasures we have
are these walks and the drink of tea which is brewed on our return; in fact, I
almost feel human again.*

Feb 28th *. . . The Nip officer, Lt. Sito, who is i/c welfare of all POW
camps in this area came today and gave us our February pay and then in the
afternoon gave us a lecture on how the rations are obtained and invited
questions. According to him, we receive about 25% more rice than the
civilians and this was causing grumbling, whilst our meat ration was double
that of the japs. Kinnear rather put his foot in it by asking if all Japs always
felt hungry!! That was not well received . . . The officers' table tennis team
beat the cookhouse by 11:5. The impression we gained from questioning Sito
was that the Japs were having a pretty thin time as everything was 'very
difficult'; apparently no silk is being made as the factories have been turned
over to war work, cotton is very scarce and wool unobtainable – whilst beer,
sake and whisky, once very plentiful, are practically impossible to obtain.*

Mar 1st *The men are moaning again against the officers and themselves
and one corporal went so far as to try and get a petition sent to the Japs for
two of the servers to be sent down the mine. They complain that we are
stealing rice(!!!) and are doing nothing towards helping them, both of which*

Lieutenant Kinnear,
RNVR. Moroyama,
January 1943.

are completely untrue. I cannot understand their mentality to go whining to some wretched ex padi-coolie on every possible occasion and still expect us to wait on them hand and foot.

Mar 2nd *Weather better today so went for another ramble round the rocks in the afternoon, having spent the morning playing table tennis . . . Sickness is very much on the increase in the camp, the mine being responsible for most of this and the sallow complexion and peaked features of those who go down the mine stands out in vivid contrast to the more rosy complexion of the surface workers . . .*

Mar 3rd *I wrote a letter to 'Chui' today requesting permission to buy sake and 'cakes' for a spree on my birthday and once again he turned up trumps, giving me a chit which enable me to buy a bottle of sake and about 2lbs of Turkish delight. If I can lay hands on any sugar I shall make a punch with the aid of the grapefruit we get, but in any case I can at least celebrate the occasion. By and large, we cannot really grumble about conditions here as we do get quite a lot of perks and certainly get far more freedom than I ever expected to get and have far more comforts than we ever had in Java. Still, I suppose it is one of our prerogatives to grouse.*

Mar 4th *Well, this is the first birthday I have spent as a prisoner of war and although it is possibly the grimmest I have had, I still managed to enjoy it. It was very pleasant to be wakened by somebody wishing me many happy returns – everybody in the room remembered – and in the mess too congratulations were offered by everybody except the Colonel, but then, he is past bothering about. At night, we had a party with the Sgt. Maj. and the rest of the members of the room, which was a huge success, the Sgt. Maj. waxing very loquacious on the sake and telling innumerable amusing anecdotes of his life in the army. A few days ago, Whitty, whilst carting pig-shit out to the garden had the misfortune of getting a tub of this over him which neither improved his looks, smell nor temper!!!!*

Mar 5th *Orderly officer again today. Spent the afternoon writing a letter to Elizabeth and also sent a card to the folks. Have been feeling rather restless of late and have been wracking my brains trying to think of some feasible means of getting out of here but always run up against the same old difficulties, namely, language, being white, lack of outside contacts and being imprisoned on an island. Supposing I could speak the lingo, it would be impossible to disguise myself as a Nip as my build would give me away at once and although there are plenty of small craft on the beach, there is nothing suitable for a long sea voyage. Perhaps, later on, an opportunity will present itself so I'm not giving up hope . . .*

Mar 6th *Went out into the garden today and spent about an hour putting manure (very smelly variety) on the soil till the supply was exhausted. Poor*

*old Mac managed to get splashed in the face with it and had just finished
blinding about this when he stepped into a furrow which had just been filled!
Whilst out there, the local photographer came along and took us. Having
finished the manuring we sat down in the sun on the cliff top and watched
the fishing fleet; presently one of the boats came inshore and I got the bright
idea of buying some fish from them; our guard was quite agreeable but unfortunately they had no fish on board. Felt rather seedy in the afternoon so went
to bed and had a long sleep. After dinner Hutch came along to the cubby-hole
and started yarning about his experiences in Malaya and Java which passed
the time very nicely. I have managed to buy a wrist watch for Y15.00 so once
again I have 'time on my hands'.*

Left to right: Pilot
Officer Bairstow,
Captain Maclean,
Captain Duncan,
Lieutenant Morton
RNR, with Jap guard,
Motoyama 1943.

Mar 7th–10th *The mines management dropped a bombshell when they
announced that there was to be no holidays for the miners during March but
magnanimously decided to give them sake instead. However, the men have
their own ideas about this and should the Col. not manage to get this readjusted I have no doubt that the men will not go without their holidays. There
has been a great deal of aerial activity of late and seaplanes have been flying
around as well as the usual fighters so perhaps some of the Jap fleet is
operating round these waters. The Japs allow the men to hold sing-songs on
Wed and Saturdays between 7pm and 9pm and there is an Irishman called
Ryan in the billet next door to us who gives a remarkably good imitation of a
female voice; last night, he suddenly started singing soprano and the sentry
who was walking up and down outside, stopped and then darted into the
billet to see who the female was!!! In the same billet are Morris and O'Neil
both of whom are absolute characters as they both hail from Glasgow and have*

been members of a razor gang the latter having a very broad accent, and the pair of them were ringleaders in the raid on the store of the ship. Have not been feeling too well of late and thought I was in for another dose of malaria last night, but happily this did not materialise. Weather much warmer now and soon we shall be able to change into tropical clothes during the daytime. I wonder how all the folks are getting on at home?

Bombadier O'Neil.

Mar 11th   The Nips have now given out instructions that postcards and letters, the latter one sheet only, have to be written in block capitals and have also changed the address so the postal business is far from satisfactory. The Col. has been arguing with Ono about holidays for the miners but does not seem to be getting very far, as Ono takes the line that the directors have ordered this measure and refuse to change it. Have been feeling rather fed up with life today and when we went onto the beach this afternoon and I saw all those fishing boats just off the shore, my thoughts once again turned to escape. If only I could hit upon some feasible method of attempting this, I would have a stab at it, but I'm not certain that these yellow swine wouldn't shoot you if you were caught and, needless to say, I don't want to throw my life away at this stage in the proceedings, as I think that another 15 months should see us free men again. Free men! I cannot think what it would be like to be your own master again; instead of being chivvied by some filthy little upstart who doesn't know the meaning of the word civilisation.

Mar 12th   There has been a great deal of fuss made over the question of letter writing, the latest 'gem' being that we have to print a card and put it into the Jap office for censoring, it is then typed by Pte. Walker – he is the only person in camp who owns a serviceable typewriter and steadfastly refuses to lend it out and then returned for signature, returned to the Japs for despatch. The subject matter is limited to health of sender, daily routine, and any other vital matter, so the scope is not great, as we are only permitted to send cards. I was so wild when this was announced that I wrote out a card using as many obscure words and phrases I could think of, and forwarded it for censoring, hoping that they would spend a pleasant time trying to find out what it was all about. Such words as 'post prandial constitutional perambulations' must have given them a great deal of food for thought. Another man has been put in clink for giving cheek to the Japs. Felt pretty bloody in the evening so retired to bed before supper.

Mar 13th   Still feeling pretty raw today and suspect a mild dose of 'flu which seems to be going the rounds; however, I got up after breakfast as I don't want to give in to it, as it is no joke being SIQ (sick in quarters). The Nips in the village have become very air raid conscious and are putting paper over the windows. A fat lot of good that will do against blast!!! We received our photos today and the results are quite good, although I must admit we

> *look a pretty desperate crowd in our motley attire . . . Morton said, 'We appear to be living on Bushido these days,' and he is not far wrong as our rations have been drastically curtailed. Still, I suppose it is a good sign and we can expect even less as time passes.*
>
> *Mar 14th–16th   The delegate of the International Red Cross, Monsieur Paravacini, who is Swiss Minister to Japan paid a visit to our camp today (16th) and having had a conference with the Col. inspected our quarters. We took the opportunity of putting forward our grievances and relating our hardships on the ship – he knows that we had been on the 'Singapore Maru' – and managed to get information about our mail etc. Apparently our names and present address is being radioed home by the IRC Intell. Bureau so that point is now clear, but we are to be allowed to send only six letters home per year, and that is far from satisfactory.*

I am grateful to Mr Philip Chinnery of NEXPOWA, the National Ex-Prisoner of War Association, who sent me photocopies of the IRC reports following a visit he made to the Public Record Office at Kew. The extracts that I quote here are from the telegram sent from M Paravacini to the IRC in London, dated 2 April 1943 and marked as received the following day:

'Camp Motoyama. Between Ohama and Ube twenty metres altitude capacity two hundred strength onesixnought including sixteen officers. Age twentyone to fortysix average thirtythree. Total area fortyone acres prisoners' barracks cover fourteen acres average twelve men in partitioned rooms . . .'

It goes on to give details of drainage of site, daily rations and medical problems encountered, finishing with a request for more cigarettes:

'. . . patients two decilitres of milk per day and more fruits. Gastroenteritis two, colds four, beriberi two, arthritis three, otitis one, phlebitis one, working accidents two . . . piece work system tried out at present. Eight working hours and two hours on way to and from mines too much. Desire more rest and recreation, more underwear, socks, towels, repair materials, books, first aid material also British Doctor and Padre if possible more contact with outside world also more things to sell in canteen more cigarettes.'

It took a month for this information from the IRC finally to get to the relatives of the POW, coming as it did via the War Office in Britain. On May 13th 1943 Atholl's family were notified by telegram that he was now known to be a prisoner of war. The following month his parents received word from the War Organisation of the British Red Cross and the Order of St John of Jerusalem (see letter, Chapter 8, p. 145) informing them that he was a prisoner in Fukuoka camp.

March 14th–16th   *I suppose they got us to write our previous letters in the hopes that they would get material for propaganda. A typical gesture on the part of the Japs, both cheap and nasty. It also appears that there are plenty of Red Cross supplies lying at Lorenco Marques but the Japs do not have the ships to send and collect this; it's pretty hard on us but I suppose it is a good sign. The cookhouse staff instituted a rat hunt – there are hundreds of rats about the camp – but their only score was one rat and two near misses, but an amusing time was had by all – with the possible exception of the rats. Absolutely no news in the papers at all these days so I'm wondering just what is going on in the outside world, and if the second front has been launched in Europe yet or not.*

March 17th–19th   *Nothing much doing over this period except a long walk we had on the 18th; going up to the top of the hill and down the other side into Anoda City and from there back to camp by way of the coast passing through Ohama and the village in which W/Cdr. Matthews' camp is situated. While passing through that village we met two of the men and had a chat with them. Evidently Blaikie, Millan, Dukes and Exley are all thriving and the men themselves looked very fit and well.*

March 20th–24th   *The Nips have been making a nuisance of themselves again and have decreed that officers must work in the garden or do fatigues and just to show that they meant business had four of us down to the pithead collecting wood on a small handcart. Of course, they would have to go and pinch all our gardening implements just to make things awkward for us. One of the men has been given nine days in the 'cooler' for smoking down the mine and deserves every day of it for he was endangering the lives of the whole shift. Mac was the victim of rather a good practical joke tonight when it was his turn to make the porridge. While he was out collecting bowls from the mess, the brazier containing the glowing charcoal on which the pot was placed was changed, an empty brazier being substituted. On his return, Mac kept watch over the pot for*

Flying Officer E. Trillwood RAFVR. Motoyama, January 1943.

about 15 minutes making sundry remarks about 'a watched pot never boils' before he discovered what had been done . . .Unfortunately there has been a good deal of theft going on in the camp, and Trillwood's office was burgled recently. I wish we could catch the swine who is doing it for it is despicable to steal from your comrades at any time, but doubly so in circumstances such as these.

March 25th   . . . The Nips have been siezed with a shrub and tree planting mania and have had the surface workers busy on this job round about the blocks in the camp and I must admit that they are an improvement. Another craze in the camp these days is pipe making, Keith having started this, through bringing back some cherry-wood branches from the garden and burning out a bowl in a short length of this with a red hot poker; I have made one for myself and am quite pleased with the result.

March 26th   . . . The local rag has been making a great song and dance over the arrival of Ba Maw in this country (PM Burma) and of his being given a decoration by the emperor and old Bird made the following remark in the mess tonight, 'I see that old Baw Bee has been made a golden shite!' I wonder what the Nips would say if they knew that the 'Grand Order of the Golden Kite' was so described. O'Neil and Morris have started up in the laundry business, and I have a flat contract rate of Y2.00 per month with them; they make a very good job of the clothes and effect small repairs such as darning socks, mending shirts etc, this being part of the service. I have been suffering from rather nasty headaches of late and put this down to eye trouble. In connection with this, I have repeatedly asked to be allowed to see the oculist in Ube but have had no satisfaction.

March 27th–28th   I have now been a captive behind barbed wire for a year and looking back over my experiences feel that I have a lot to be thankful for, as I am still alive and am reasonably fit and feel that the worst is over. It seems a long long time since I was last free and, looking ahead, I cannot think of any date on which I can look forward to my release, but somehow, I think that it is not too far distant and am quite content to live from day to day. We often talk about past experiences in the mess after meals, and only tonight we were discussing the wireless and the gestapo's efforts to trace this in Priok, as well as the carrier pigeon 'service'. The troops have discovered a new method of taking a 'rise' out of the Japs who insist that roll-call shall be carried out in Japanese. The last bit of this is 'Ijo arimasen' pronounced 'Ee joe arry-ma-sen' but most of troops look the Jap NCO straight in the face and then say very deliberately, 'Is you 'arry Mason?'!! I am looking forward to hearing some news about the opening of the second front some day soon, and feel that once this is got under way it won't be long before Germany packs up.

March 29th–31st   Rather a nasty incident took place today . . . one of the men received a leg injury down the mine a few days ago and has been confined to bed with it, was dragged out of bed by the Nips and hauled off to the guard-room where he was beaten up with sticks so badly that his cries could be heard all over the camp. The Japs allege that four days ago down the mine he turned to one of the Koreans, gave the 'thumbs up' sign and said, 'Koreans OK' then drew a map of Japan in the mud and spat on it. The Nips also claim that he confessed to this after a while; at present he has been given 8 days solitary. All our issue leather boots have been withdrawn, no reason being given for this but as all the army guards are leaving tomorrow perhaps they are to be supplied with footgear at our expense...

April 1st–3rd   Our new guards who are employees of the mine are an absolute shower and have been making themselves very unpopular by strutting about the camp, finding fault with everything and demanding salutes when they are not entitled to them. Ever since Paravacini visited the camp the Japs have been very hostile towards us and one of them told Trilwood that they were very annoyed about what we told him; evidently they expected us to say how well we were being treated etc, etc, and did not like an outsider to learn the true facts about the conditions under which we are living...I'm quite certain that when we are released from here, there will be many incidents of Japs getting beaten up and they will richly deserve it; I have got two slaps in the face to even up and fully intend to clout somebody good and hard before I leave this god-forsaken land. From today, I am going to keep a record of all books that I want to read whenever I get the chance.

One of many lists that he made in his notebooks.

April 4th–9th   *Very little to report over this period as it has been raining heavily most of the time with the result that we have been cooped up in our hovels...I took the opportunity presented by the wet weather to get my narrative transferred to a notebook and amended it adding quite a lot to certain parts; so far I have not attempted to write up about Priok as a lot of facts about that place might still be useful to the 'yellow brethren'.*

April 10th–13th   *The Nips have announced that Paravacini is paying another visit to this camp on the 16th and their changed attitude towards us of late has been very noticeable. Out in the garden, there is a great deal to be done in the way of planting and weeding but as the weather has been very cold with a high wind, work out there has been far from pleasant of late and the sentries have shown a marked reluctance to go out, inventing all sorts of excuses to get out of it. We went for a walk today and coming back down the hillside behind the school, the guard and Mac lagged behind. Suddenly the sentry stopped, handed Mac his rifle and vanished into a back garden where he started to pick flowers while old Mac was left on the path with a rifle in his hands, not knowing quite what to do with it when a civilian came round a corner and saw him there, apparently guarding the path, swallowing quickly twice he disappeared back the way he had come, going like a scalded cat!!!*

April 14th–16th   *The Col. has been given five days solitary for the alleged Murikami affair, this news being sprung on us on the evening before the Swiss was due to arrive. He is not allowed to smoke or read, having to sit in his room all day facing a sentry and no one is allowed to speak to him. Obviously this is a move to get him out of the way for the inspection, being a typical Japanese trick. When the Swiss arrived he kicked up quite a row about the whole affair and showed a decided anti-Jap attitude, contradicting the Major who accompanied him on more than one occasion. He again told us not to expect any more Red Cross supplies as the Japs were not in a position to collect them, and stressed the fact that there was yards and yards of red tape up in Tokyo, but also said that we were very fortunate in our accommodation as the POW camps in Osaka and Kobe were wretched shacks inside factories, the inmates having no eiderdowns or blankets supplied and also had no opportunity of getting fresh air. When the question of holidays for the miners arose he said he could do nothing as this was purely a local matter but added that there had been a 'serious incident' in Ube over this matter last month. By the way, it was not Paravacini who came but a Monsieur Kengelbacher who was a member of the Swiss delegation in Tokyo. He also told us that the war was being waged 'very strongly', this being taken to mean in our favour, and that mail had arrived in this country, but that the Japs would not release it for distribution as their POW lists were not complete. Another point about this conference was the fact that all the senior officers were forbidden to interview him and only Trilwood was to be permitted to speak to him. I have been getting on quite well with the book of late and have started to write up about Priok and find that there is no end of material in this phase of our life…one of the men is in clink and is being beaten up pretty frequently by these yellow swine but refuses to be subdued. Poor lad, he's having a pretty rough time of it, but some day, our turn will come and God help these rats then.*

The diary continues in a new notebook and the following are the first couple of pages of notes made before his next move. He starts off by explaining the reason that they are not dated.

Since I last made an entry in my diary a great deal has come to pass and altho' a great deal has slipped my memory, I'll try to set down the salient points. The first thing that occurred at Motoyama after my last entry was that we were forbidden to keep diaries and all that were in our possession had to be turned in for censorship so we told the Japs that all diaries had been destroyed – which they had not been – and limited entries – keeping the books well out of sight.

This act of defiance must have been a boost to his morale, restoring a sense of control, an essential ingredient in his battle to survive.

One day, the Japs told us that they considered that the garden was too big for us to manage and that they were going to take over a portion of it; naturally, the area that they appropriated was that in which all the potatoes were, and as these were just about ripe for digging up, our feelings about this can well be imagined. Towards the end of June, the weather became very hot and we requested permission to go bathing but this was refused by Chui; however we managed to persuade some of the guards to let us have a dip when we went out for walks. About the middle of July, Trillwood got wind of a move for some of the officers so I took steps to conceal the various documents I had in my kit and it is just as well that I did, for on the 26th we were informed that the Col., Major Campbell, Keith, Paul, Mac, Kinnear and self were being transferred to another camp and were to have our kits laid out for

Major Emmett, RA. Motoyama, January 1943.

inspection after lunch on the following day. Very fortunately I was able to buy a suitcase from Maj. Emmett, as I would not have been able to transport my various belongings in the packs etc which I then possessed as I had bought a fair amount of kit from those who wished to part with it.

This last sentence always makes me smile. It conjures up a wonderful picture in my mind of a ragged, half-starved prisoner of war being accompanied by a porter carrying his luggage!

It was so like the man I knew not only to have acquired so many useful possessions but to have contrived a way of transporting them. In later life his instinct to collect anything of interest or possible use eventually became more obsessive in nature and caused many difficulties at home.

When the time came for the inspection, it was far more rigorous than I had expected and as I was afraid that my diaries etc would be discovered, I substituted harmless packs for those containing my jottings. The next snag was that all kit, once it had been checked had to be repacked under the watch of a sentry and stowed away overnight in the guardroom, but I was able to effect the change over of the packs once again, with the aid of Keith, under their very noses. On the day that we left Motoyama (28th July) our Red Cross boots were confiscated by the Japs, their reason for this being that the boots were camp property and so we could not take them away: Maj. Campbell was obliged to make the journey in a pair of tattered canvas shoes. Chui had said that he was going to present us with some food for the journey and, much to our surprise, produced two tins of salmon, a small amount of sugar and 'butter' – about ¼ lb of each of the last two, and we were marvelling at this amazing burst of generosity on his part right up till the time we were paid and then we discovered that his little treat had cost each of us Y11.00 or a total of Y77.00 for the whole lot. After the elaborate precautions that they had taken to check our kit we fully expected that our washing and toilet kit would be searched when we replaced it in our baggage but such was not the case and here again some of us were able to smuggle in extras. Before I go on to describe the journey, I'll make mention of two incidents one rather humorous and the other decidedly not. One day, the Japs decided that we should hold a fire drill and so paraded us out on the square and divided us up into squads, each squad having a jap NCO i/c. We were told that when the alarm sounded we were to proceed to the scene of the fire and extinguish it 'quam celerime'. On the bugle sounding, we all set off at high speed and just before we turned the corner to go down past the cookhouse, one of the long bamboo poles with short lengths of rope tied on the end, was thrust against the back of Willie Wetlegs' neck and I heard a voice say, 'Take that, you bastard.' Willie could not get his neck free from this thing as our boy could run faster than he could and was screaming Japanese invective at the top of his voice until he was slapped up against the boundary fence! When we got to where the fire was, we discovered that it had not been lit so stood round in a semi-circle armed with buckets of water; when the carbide fire did finally get going, the Jap who was lighting it (Anoda) collected more water on his person than the fire did! Result. No more fire drills. The other incident concerns that worthy, O'Neil. One evening the Japs gave us some sake and unfortunately O'Neil got more than was good for him, and when it came time to go to bed, he became very truculent when ordered by a sentry. However, the men in the room managed to calm him down, and just as he was turning to go to bed, the sentry slapped him, whereupon O'Neil knocked the sentry through the door with an uppercut. More Japs appeared on the scene, and O'Neil was taken up to the guard-room where he was mercilessly pounded with rifle butts, being knocked down several times. As he lay on the ground he wailed, 'Friends, Friends' but as soon as he got to his feet, he would yell, 'I murder you, you yellow b—s.' Finally he was thrown into the cooler where he spent the night and was released the following morning when we explained to Chui that he was drunk and did not know what he was doing.

The men had been having a pretty miserable time at the hands of the Japs as these would parade up and down the corridors collecting salutes and handing out slaps here, there and everywhere but had been feeling very optimistic about the prospect of an early release as our offensives in Sicily and the Solomons had been going very well . . . Whilst on the topic of food, I will say that the food we were receiving was ample as regards the needs of the officers who did not do any heavy work but was not sufficient for the men who had to work pretty strenuously down the mine, and the Japanese were going to stop the system of piece work and were going to keep the men below the surface for the full shift period – but the men had their own ideas on this and I know that their output would considerably decrease as a result of such a measure. An interesting fact about the mine was that women – probably Korean – were being used and these used to work alongside their men folk; one of the men was given a spell in the cooler for propositioning one of these the agreed price being seven yen!!! For Whitsun we decided to kill one of the pigs and when the time came, the cookhouse sallied forth to do the execution, Gertie being the unhappy victim as when the boar had been brought to her, she led him an awful dance and ended up by

ID photograph taken at Motoyama, January 1943.

> *biting his pills refusing to let him do anything. Unfortunately, the Japs got wind of what was happening and as they wished to see another 'exhibition' and we were equally determined that they wouldn't, they took their revenge by beating up all the cookhouse staff, Bird getting clouted as well, just for good measure but when the meals were served one and all agreed that they had been well worth it, and as the Col. said as we ate our banquet from a table complete with cloth etc. 'If that stupid pig had not been so sexually frigid she would have been alive now.'*

Below is the menu that Dad kept from the meal. In addition to being a good example of prisoner of war humour, it is an interesting document. Among the signatories is Pilot Officer Bird, the individual who got clouted in the previous paragraph. His signature is second from bottom right-hand column. I know of one other copy of this document. It is held at the Imperial War Museum. That one bears my father's signature – it belonged to Pilot Officer Bird. I wonder how many more of these menus are still in existence?

DINER PENTECOTE
-oOo-

1. Cotelette Mlle. Gertie Vierge
   au grand jamais.
2. Sauce Larmes aux Ye ux.
3. Pommes rotis.
4. Pommess Duchesse aux Fukien
   officiers.
5. Petits pois a l'air eclatant.
6. Haricots Excrement de Taureau.
7. Choux Motoyama.
8. Pudding embonpoint.
9. Poires Croix Rouge a la
   Mathilde Valsante.
10. Pain Mickey.
11. Thé Bushido Evanoui.

Officers' Mess,
Motoyama P.O.W Camp,
Whitsunday, 6th June 1943.

Returning to the diary:

Getting back to the subject of our move, we had been told that we were going to a very nice place in the island of Shikoku but we had heard such stories before and did not place a great deal of faith in them. On the 28th July just after lunch we got the word to move and having piled our baggage on a truck, set out for the station where we boarded the electric train and were taken to Ube and dumped in what appeared to be a military school where several other officers from camps in the vicinity were already arrived. In our wanderings trying to find this place we had been taken to Col. Scott's camp which was situated next to a huge coal distillation plant, the atmosphere here being appalling. Thank God that I had transferred from his party at Moji as we at least could breathe fresh air at Motoyama and from all accounts we had infinitely more food as the officers there had had to exist on starvation rations, pap rice being the only thing they had received in the cereal line.

He had indeed been fortunate, as the following comments were made by Kengelbacher, the Swiss envoy and IRC delegate, in the official report to the International Red Cross Committee about camp No. 7 (Col. Scott's camp at Ube). He visited the camps in mid-April 1943, one month after Paravacini, and his observations bear out Atholl's misgivings about the camp at Ube:

'. . . not specially complaining but somehow prisoners not looking healthy, being overworked – underfed . . . Summing up, all the Fukuoka camps (but No. 7) can be considered reasonably satisfactory.'

The diary continues:

For eight hours we had to wait there, and although we were not supposed to talk to people other than those in our own group, we soon were exchanging details about our treatment. As far as I have been able to ascertain, we had been very fortunate, most camps being much worse than ours as regards food clothing and recreation, and I was horrified to hear the rest of the story about the 'Singapore Maru'. Evidently approximately 400 sick had been left on board when we left the ship and these had been left to fend for themselves for three days, receiving no medical attention, their food being dumped on the deck so that they could get it if they were able and if not, they went without. By the time that the Japs decided to do something for them 110 had died and of the remaining who went to hospitals in and around Moji, approximately 225 died. Of the supposedly fit personnel who went to the camps between 70–100 had died so that the total death-roll came to more than 331, 33% of our number when we left Singapore. At 1930 that evening we were loaded onto motor vehicles and taken to the mainline station about 10 km outside Ube where we caught the Moji-Tokyo express. Our accommodation was not too bad – being 3rd class – but as the seats were made to accommodate 4 Japs we were cramped for space as their average stature is much smaller than ours. After an overnight journey, we detrained at a small port opposite the north of Shikoku and carried our baggage to the grounds of a small shrine beside the harbour where we had to wait for four hours till the ferry arrived. Here we were given a slice of bread; some Japanese savouries, and a cup of green tea, a similar amount being issued as a ration for our lunch and while we ate our frugal meal, it seemed that all Japan came to watch us eat. At ten thirty we boarded the ferry and were herded below decks to a large cabin with the usual straw matting on the floor and having eaten my lunch I fell asleep for the remainder of the voyage. When we disembarked, the Jap Lieut. who was i/c informed us that we had a five mile hike to the station so we told him that we could not possibly make it carrying our luggage and much to our surprise he hired an ox-cart and got the luggage put on his while we walked to the station of the port which was called Todatsu. Here we boarded another train and after about a quarter hour journey reached the town of Zentsuji where we detrained and once again hired a bullock cart for the baggage and after about a mile's hike reached our new home which was an old army barracks where the German prisoners in the last war had been housed during their stay in Japan, and where there were already quite a few American, Australian and British prisoners, of all services.'

It was the end of July 1943. He had been in captivity for sixteen months and still had no word from home.

Chapter 8

The War of Words at Home

1942–1943

The autumn and winter of 1942 were long and tiring for everyone in the Duncan and Glassey families. Despite the return of all her letters to Atholl earlier on that summer, Elizabeth had not given up hope that he was alive somewhere and she got on with her life as best she could.

From September she and Pauline Quig were sharing digs in Dundee, revising all day in the library for their re-sits in December. All that Pauline can now recall was the endless revision but Elizabeth referred to those months in a letter to Atholl dated 15/7/43 when she said,

> 'Pauline and I were in the same digs for the last term in Dundee – we stayed in Airlie Terrace above where Nesta lived. It was very convenient for the library where we almost lived but the bunk-wife was an awful twister and I was mighty glad to get out.'

The only one of her returned letters that has survived, dated 12 February 1942, was addressed to the new British HQ at Lembang near Bandoeng in the mountains of Dutch-controlled Java.

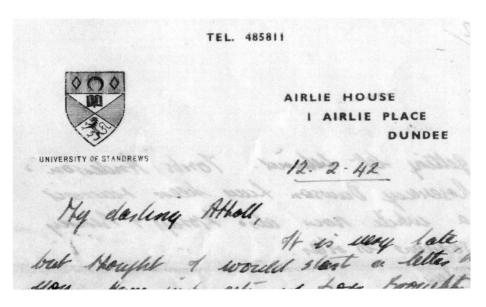

The only letter from Elizabeth to Atholl from 1942 which has survived.

Envelope for Elizabeth's letter which was returned. Note address in Java overstamped with non-delivery message.

In it she chatted about life and student friends of theirs getting engaged, one notably to a 'flashy dame!' She told him about her hospital experiences; standing around in a hot theatre during endlessly long operating lists, her feet swollen and legs aching after hours with nothing to lean on (good training for the future). Half way through the letter, noting that it was now Tuesday 17 February she wrote,

> 'Bunty (his sister) phoned me last night and told me the wonderful news of your promotion. I can't tell you how pleased I feel and it has only been with great restraint that I haven't rushed up to everyone I met in the street and told them the good news. You must be doing your work very well indeed to get promoted so soon – specially as some people seem to wait a life-time and then never get it – still they are not you!! It was the most wonderful news I have heard for ages and am I proud!!'

After a couple more sides, in which she reminded him of happier times when her brother Billy had holidayed with them in Scotland and the fun they had all had, she seemed to have a premonition of what was to come for she signed off the letter with these prophetic words:

> 'Well I must close this long drawn out epistle and post it. It is only an extra and probably will never reach you for months, if then.'

Back to the closing stages of 1942 and life everywhere was so fraught. In Bradford, the Glasseys were not just concerned about Elizabeth and her fiancé, but they were also worried about Billy, who had finally been called to join the Naval Volunteer Reserve and in October had sailed as a Surgeon Lieutenant on HMS *Striker*, his whereabouts unknown for the foreseeable future.

Letter from Billy to his mother.

> 19.12.42.
>
> 15th letter
>
> H.M.S *Striker*
> ℅ G.P.O
> London.
>
> Dear Mum,
>
> It was very nice to get a letter from you, directly after the 2 from Dad. Yours arrived on Wednesday. Thank you for the cable. You can always get in touch with me by that method, even if I have left the Hotel, as they would probably send it on.
>
> Sorry to hear that there is no news of Atholl. but have a feeling he is O.K.

Envelope with Brooklyn postmark.

Friends of the Glassey's had already received the worst news of all about their son and the family doctor was anxiously awaiting news of his boy who was also missing in the Far East. In time Dr West-Watson received news that his son was a prisoner of war. By an astonishing coincidence, Lieutenant West-Watson eventually turned up at Zentsuji where he later wrote his name and address in one of Dad's pocket books along with dozens of other fellow prisoners of all nationalities.

Lieutenant West-Watson's name and address as it appears in Atholl's pocket book along with dozens of other prisoners' contact details.

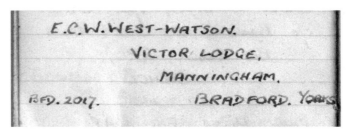

Over half a century later, in 1998, during my interview with Mr Suddaby at the Imperial War Museum, I was shown a newly-published book written by R. Keith Mitchell. *Forty-two Months in Durance Vile* is an account of his prisoner of war experiences in Singapore and Japan. Among the photographic plates in the book there is a propaganda picture taken in December 1943 which features a group of British and Dutch officers at Muroran camp in northern Japan. Lieutenant West-Watson is clearly visible and named in the caption alongside.

As 1942 drew to a close, life was no less tense for the Duncan family in St Andrews since, in addition to the daily worry of Atholl's whereabouts and safety, there was the business to keep going in spite of the shortages of supplies and manpower. In July of the previous year, Atholl's father had secured a contract from the British Overseas Airways Corporation (BOAC) to continue the supply of motor transport for personnel at RAF Leuchars (see page 18). The invoice opposite, for work carried out in 1943 is evidence of the continuing reliance each had on the other.

It was a very significant contract not only for the health of his business but also for the war effort. Vital fuel and spare part supplies would be required by the garage to continue providing these services and this would inevitably prove to be helpful to other customers. But more importantly, the smooth running of the work of the RAF station would continue uninterrupted. RAF Leuchars played a pivotal role during the war years in more ways than one. Sweden (a neutral country) was trading with both Britain and Germany and it was vital that regular communication was maintained. To this end, BOAC operated a small courier fleet of Mosquitoes between Leuchars and Stockholm. In accordance with international law they had to be civil-registered, hence the BOAC involvement. The bomb-bays of these aircraft were converted to carry a passenger, mail and cargo. The British purchased Sweden's entire output of ball-bearings,

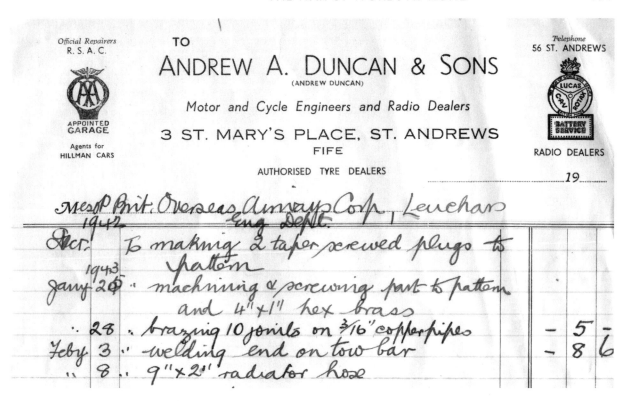

Invoice relating to work carried out for BOAC.

principally to prevent the Germans getting hold of them, and much of this cargo passed through Leuchars, along with priority passengers and diplomatic mail.

Early in 1943 Atholl's father was involved in a very serious incident (connected with this contract) while on a business trip to Edinburgh. He was suspected of being a SPY! Once the matter had been resolved and he could see there was a funny side to the incident, Andrew committed the facts to paper for posterity, using the pseudonym 'Sandy'. I found his hand-written account of the story carefully filed in a folder marked '1939 – 45' in which he had kept all his correspondence and documentation applicable to that period. The following is an extract from his account:

'I'll call him Sandy, although that is not his real name, which, in fact, is as Scottish as a name can be and Sandy was as Scottish as his name implied. He had all the characteristic qualities of the typical Scot – a little dour at times; quite determined in his ways; loyal to his ideals and friends; rather quiet; athletic and sound in his views. And yet during the 1939-45 war, Sandy was accused of being a spy! No one who knew him would have dreamt of such a thing happening, and no one could, I am sure, have credited such a charge being made. But happen it did.

Actually Sandy was the proprietor of a cycle and motor business, which his father had founded in the nineties, and which he also helped to build

and had expanded. During the war years, supplies of repair parts and acces-
sories were difficult . . . necessitating going into one of the larger cities and
visiting the various wholesaler warehouses and sometimes getting odd parts
from the dealers in scrapped cars. On one of such outings about 1943 he
was spotted by a young woman, who thought she recognised him as a guide
she had met in Germany. So she followed him; took careful notes of his
doings and finally reported her findings and her suspicions to the Police
Authorities in this large city. Her report was carefully checked, and the
various warehouses gave Sandy's name and confirmed that he had been
there at the times mentioned.

Next morning Sandy was surprised to receive a call at his place of
business from the local Inspector of Police, whom he knew well, for Sandy
was a Special Constable! The Inspector asked to see him in private. When
they adjourned to Sandy's office, the Inspector seemed a little ill at ease and
said he didn't like doing what he had to do and saying what he had to say,
so Sandy told him not to worry, but just to tell him why he had called...and
the Inspector explained he had had an urgent phone call from the police in
the large city, instructing him to get answers to their questions from the
suspect without delay. And if the answers were in the affirmative, would he
arrange for Sandy to call at their Police Headquarters for an interview, and
to be inspected by their informer?

. . . Sandy was naturally furious, and at first refused to go. Then he
calmed down a little, and said he would go if all his expenses and his time
were paid for... he was courteously received by the Detective Inspector and
then the accuser was brought into the room. She eyed Sandy from every
angle, and she even stood at his back to compare heights. She was positive
she had met him in Germany in 1938 – he had been the guide to their party
then! Sandy retorted he had never been in Germany at anytime, had no
German connections, knew no German either as a language or as individuals, and then added was it likely that he would do anything to assist our
enemies, when his son had fought in France and after coming thro'
Dunkirk had been sent to Singapore to join the forces there and was now
posted missing? There were several exchanges . . . the woman still persisting
in her views that Sandy was a spy, tho' her face by now was rather red. The
Detective Inspector then remarked that in his opinion she had made a
mistake – an honest mistake no doubt – but he was quite convinced of
Sandy's innocence . . . it was a difficult time, and everyone had to be on
guard – but this time a blunder had been made . . . the Inspector expressed
his regrets and thanks to Sandy for clearing up matters so quickly and satis-
factorily – but it just shows you what can happen.'

It must have seemed like the last straw to Special Police Constable 98, businessman and elder of the Town Kirk, but such were the risks attached to going about your daily business in times of war, yet another stress to be dealt with.

Atholl's older sister Bunty, who lived with her parents, had worked as a children's nurse pre-war and later trained as a secretary. During the war she worked at the garage with her father. In addition she was kept busy with war work in the town helping out at the canteen set up for the Polish airmen. These were members of the Polish Air Force who had managed to escape to Britain. They were stationed at nearby RAF Leuchars but billeted all over St Andrews and the surrounding area. Whenever time allowed she would also try and help out her older sister, Nesta, who lived a few miles away in Newport, near Dundee. Nesta had met George Robertson at university when he was studying medicine and they married in 1939. He went on to serve in the Army Medical Corps in West Africa, while Nesta looked after their baby son, also George, who was by then two years old.

Bunty nursing one of her charges – in the mid-1930s.

In those days people kept in touch with each other by letter especially when telephone communications were so disrupted. There would have been several deliveries each day and these must have been anticipated and feared in almost equal measure in practically every household. Urgent messages were sent by telegram and they too struck fear in the heart despite often bringing good news. Much of the Duncan family correspondence from this period has survived and it provides a fascinating insight into life both at home and abroad during the war years.

One family friend who corresponded regularly was Alec Rattray, Andrew's old school friend, whom Atholl and his sisters knew as 'Uncle Alick' (I use the spelling 'Alec' as this is how Dad referred to him throughout the diary, though, the man signed himself 'Alick' in his letters).

Alec was born in Dundee on 15 January 1986 and had emigrated to North America in 1924, settling in California, where he and his wife Elly brought up their family, two boys named Alexander (Sonny) and Danny in the city of San José.

Alec and Elly Rattray. This photo was sent to Andrew and Amelia in 1951. It was taken at Sonny's wedding in San José, California.

In his letter to Andrew, dated 23 December 1942, he was anxious for news of Atholl so that he could send parcels and he also told the family that Atholl was now registered with the American Red Cross.

Meanwhile, at about this time back in Dundee, Elizabeth and Pauline learned that they had been successful and both were at last fully qualified doctors. Elizabeth returned to her parents' home for the festivities and spent part of the holidays helping out as a locum at one of the hospitals in Bradford.

Letter from Alec
Rattray to Atholl's
parents.

UNITED STATES PRODUCTS CORPORATION, LTD.

D. C. KOK
PRESIDENT

CABLE ADDRESS
"UNIPROCOR"
CODES
CALPAK — BENTLEYS
A.B.C. 5TH AND 6TH ED.
ARMSBY   C.F.C.A.

P.O. BOX 256
RACE ST. AT MOORPARK AVE.
SAN JOSE, CALIFORNIA

December 23rd 1942.

My Dear Andy, Millie, and all the Family;-

I feel a sort of guilty in not answering your fine long letter of
some weeks ago, and can offer no excuse other than I did not seize the
chances to write when I should. First of all we were all glad and happy
that Atholl at least got out of Singapore, and pray and hope that he will
be all right even though the Jap now has the Dutch East Indies. I immediatley scouted around for a Geographic Magazine relative to the Indies
and mailed same to you some time ago in order that you would have a better
idea of the land he was located in. We all have a inner feeling that he
will be all right and that as everything usually turns out for the best
it may prove to be that he is now safe until such time as the war is all
finished. Should you receive any word I would appreciate if you would let
me know right away and if I can send a parcel through the American Red
Cross I would immediatley do so. I am enclosing a cutting from our local new
paper of a local marriage that of two St Andrews Students who must have
attended there when Atholl or Nesta did. I wrote a note care of the base
which is about 14 miles from here inviting both the Bride and Groom to

Letter to Atholl's father
from the Netherlands
Colonial Office in
London –
4 January 1943.

MINISTERIE
VAN KOLONIËN

(Netherlands Colonial Office)

No. 1056/VIII 27.

Re: Capt. Andrew
Atholl Duncan.

STRATTON HOUSE,
STRATTON STREET, W. 1

LONDEN, 4 Januari 1943

Mr. Andrew Duncan,
Mansefield,
St. Andrews.

Dear Sir,

With reference to your letter of December 26th 1942 asking
for information about your son Capt. Andrew Atholl Duncan, Argyll
and Sutherland Highlanders, attached to the G.H.Q at Bandoeng, Java,
I regret to inform you that in this Department nothing is known of
his whereabouts.

As, due to the Japanese occupation, there is no communication
with the Netherlands East Indies., we are unable to make any inquiries
yet.

The only thing we can say is that all forces in Java, must be
assumed now to be prisoners of war in Japanese hands.

After a brief return to St Andrews for her graduation (when she and her mother stayed with Atholl's parents), she started her first post-registration job as a House Officer (in surgery) at St Luke's, Bradford's municipal hospital in mid-January 1943.

In his never-ending quest for information about his son, Andrew had sat down on Boxing Day 1942 and written to the Ministerie Van Kolonien (Netherlands Colonial Office) in London, asking for their assistance (see opposite page). Early in the New Year he received a reply stating that they had no news but they would keep him posted.

The winter dragged on. Then, in mid-March the family received a second letter from the War Office Casualty Branch, based at the Blue Coat School in Liverpool, dated 11 March 1943 (six months after the first letter from this department). This time they were informed that in the absence of any news regarding the Allied forces in Java, it had been decided that their son must be posted as missing on the

Elizabeth on her graduation day – January 1943.

Tel. No. : Liverpool Wavertree 4000.

Any further communication on this subject should be addressed to :—

The Under Secretary of State,
  The War Office,
    Casualty Branch,
      Blue Coat School,
        Church Road,
          Wavertree,
            Liverpool 15.

and the following number quoted :—

....O.S.259/D............. (Casualties)

THE WAR OFFICE,
  CASUALTY BRANCH,
    BLUE COAT SCHOOL
      CHURCH ROAD,
        WAVERTREE,
          LIVERPOOL, 15.

/1 March, 1943.

Sir,

    With reference to the letter sent to you on the 26th September, 1942, explaining that, while it was not possible to communicate with personnel in Java, there was no reason to believe that your son, Captain A.A. Duncan, The Argyll and Sutherland Highlanders, was not serving in Java with the British and Allied forces still known to be fighting there, I am directed to inform you that it has been decided that, in the absence of any news of these forces, it can no longer be assumed that they are still operating.

    It is regretted, therefore, that your son must be posted as missing on the 1st February, 1943. This posting does not mean that hope that your son is still alive must be abandoned. On the contrary, he may eventually prove to be a prisoner of war in Java - like others, a number of whom have already been reported by the Japanese Authorities - or he may still be free and at large in the island. Any information relating to him that is received will be passed to you immediately.

    I am to add that the selection of the 1st February, 1943, for posting purposes is not intended to suggest that the occurrence of casualties before that particular day will not be revealed in due course.

        I am, Sir,
          Your obedient Servant,

          A. Williams

Andrew Duncan Esq.,
  Mansefield,
    St. Andrews,
      Fife.

Letter to his parents – Atholl was officially posted as missing.

1 February 1943, and it was anticipated that they would eventually be notified he was a prisoner of war in Java.

This was followed up a week later by a leaflet dated 18 March outlining various allowances that were available to dependants of officers reported missing. Next, they received a reply (dated 23 March) from the War Office to a letter Andrew had sent on 13 March. In these letters Atholl was referred to as 'Capt A. A. Duncan' which proved to be significant in the coming months as his father battled with the War Office to have his son's pay made up at the correct rate for his rank. The War Office would not recognise Atholl's promotion to Captain as it had not been gazetted – appeared in the *London Gazette* – and therefore paid him as a Lieutenant. No fewer than 17 letters pertain to this campaign on the home front.

And then, on Thursday 13 May, another telegram from the War Office arrived at the Duncan family home.

Telegram from the War Office to the Duncan family notifying them that Atholl was a prisoner of war, 13 May 1943.

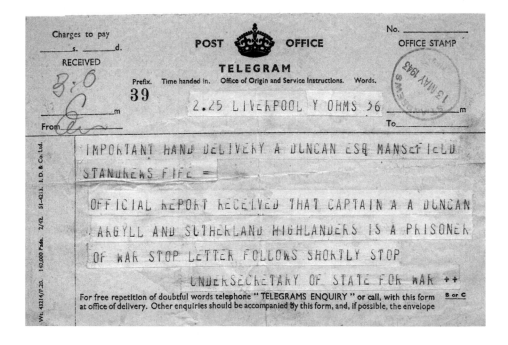

There must have been many tears of relief. Without delay Andrew sent a telegram to Elizabeth in Bradford telling her the news (opposite, top).

Word soon spread around St Andrews and there was much activity, with notices in the newspapers and well-wishers stopping them in the street or calling at Mansefield. Madras College (Atholl's old school) apparently learnt the news the same day, as a record card exists which was made out by staff, dated 13 May 1943, noting the same outline information that was given to the family. This was later added to as more details emerged. The school kept this card index pertaining to all past pupils on active service.

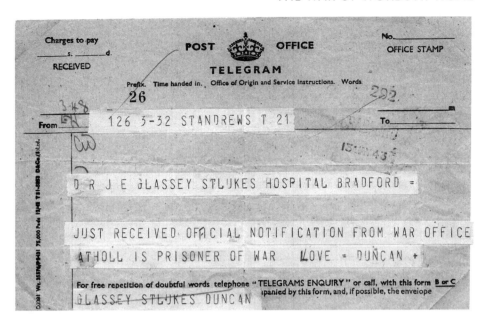

Telegram to Elizabeth from Atholl's father, 13 May 1943.

Later on, some of his teachers, as well as professors from the university, wrote to Atholl in captivity.

Andrew sent off a telegram to Alec Rattray and on Saturday morning a cable arrived from San José.

Telegram from Alec Rattray in California to the Duncan family in St Andrews, 15 May 1943.

A few days later, Alec's regular letter (usually two sides, typed on a business letterhead) arrived, having crossed with the cable.

It had been written on 12 May, the day before the wonderful news had broken. In it he outlined the industrial activity and war effort now apparent all over the West Coast, with tanks and heavy armaments stockpiled in great quantities and shipping crowding every available quayside. Now the Americans too were subject to rationing, with both sugar and coffee being hard to come by. He mentioned having sent off some *TIME* and *LIFE* magazines for Bunty and then he continued,

> 'Elly and I both hope that you have had some sort of good word about Atholl and we all hope and pray that ere long he will be back for good some day soon in your midst once again, none the worse for his many adventures.'

Once again, prophetic words. It was little surprise when, before the month was out, yet another airmail letter had arrived from San José, this time a single, typed page, dated 17 May. The Rattray family were overjoyed at the news.

On 20 May the War Office wrote, following up their telegram with more details. The family were now informed that Captain A. A. Duncan was interned in one of the 'Fukuoka Camps'. They requested that should the family receive any news from their son would they inform the authorities without delay. The government was desperately trying to account for many thousands of missing service personnel. Letters home from prisoners of war might have mentioned others and so it was imperative for families to pass on any news.

Three days later his father wrote to Elizabeth sending her details of Atholl's address and enclosing extracts about the Fukuoka camps which he had just read in a British Red Cross magazine dated April 1943. Copies of these magazines had been passed on to him by Mrs Rankin whose husband was a prisoner of war in Germany (he was one of the church ministers in St Andrews). Before too long the Red Cross were sending copies of the magazines direct to Mansefield. Atholl's father also mentioned having written to his friend in Australia, Mr Arthur Burley, asking if he too could send parcels to Atholl in Japan. Arthur was Managing Director of Berlei Ltd., (nowadays Berlei is part of Pacific Dunlop Limited) based in Sydney and well placed to be able to offer practical assistance to his Scottish friend. In his letter of reply, dated 27 July 1943, he enclosed a leaflet produced by the Australian Red Cross POW section which he had visited that morning. He offered to make up and send parcels through the ARC just as soon as permitted. His long letter ended with the following paragraph:

> 'Mrs Burley joins me in warm regards and the hope that peace with victory will soon enable this troubled world to return to sanity, and end the long separations, trials and sufferings of the millions who are now enslaved to one man's lust for power.'

During the following week the Duncans placed announcements in the personal column of *The Scotsman* (published on Friday 28 May), and in the local newspaper, the *St Andrews Citizen* (the cost for both notices being 17s 2¹/₂d).

ST ANDREWS OFFICER A PRISONER

Mr and Mrs Andrew Duncan, St Mary's Place, St Andrews, have been officially informed that their son, Captain Athol Duncan, Argyll and Sutherland Highlanders, who was reported missing as from February 1, 1943, is now a prisoner of war. Captain Duncan was a science student of St Andrews University before joining the Services.

CHURCH BELLS BROADCAST

Notice which appeared in *St Andrews Citizen* – May 1943.

There then followed an avalanche of letters to his parents, with friends and business associates from all over Scotland rejoicing with them. These simple messages of goodwill must have been a great encouragement to them all.

Next, the War Organisation of the British Red Cross Society and Order of St John of Jerusalem began to whirr into action with more details about where their son was, gleaned from the reports of the IRC visits to Japan earlier in the year (see page 101). A letter dated 11 June (quoting Atholl's reference number as FE20017) informed the family about the circulation of the Prisoner of War magazines. Handwritten on the back of this standard letter was the address of his camp, bringing a real sense of immediacy and contact to an otherwise business missive.

Address letters as follow.

PRISONER OF WAR POST
SERVICE DES PRISONNIERS DE GUERRE

100911 CAPTAIN A. A. DUNCAN
BRITISH PRISONER OF WAR
FUKUOKA CAMP.

Atholl's address written on back of letter from the Red Cross.

With the interminable months of waiting for news now over, at last they could all begin to do something to help him, even if it was only writing letters; but still they had no word from him directly.

His family and Elizabeth got copies of the official guidelines (from the Post Office) which stipulated only one typed letter a week was allowed.

The Red Cross wrote again on 1 July (see p. 147) to notify the family that from now on they would be receiving copies of the monthly magazine and, in a letter written to her brother on 3 July, Bunty told him that they were receiving these magazines.

Extract from instructions on how to address mail to POWs from the Post Office, 1943.

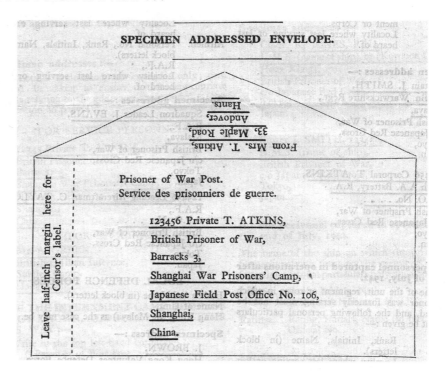

SPECIMEN ADDRESSED ENVELOPE.

From Mrs. T. Atkins,
33, Maple Road,
Andover,
Hants.

Prisoner of War Post.
Service des prisonniers de guerre.

123456 Private T. ATKINS,
British Prisoner of War,
Barracks 3,
Shanghai War Prisoners' Camp,
Japanese Field Post Office No. 106,
Shanghai,
China.

Leave half-inch margin here for Censor's label.

After so long, letter writing was not easy and they all struggled to find the right words to convey their feelings while trying to keep his spirits up and comply with censorship rules. This echoes Atholl's feelings only months earlier when he tried finding the right words to express himself.

Elizabeth started writing again on 1 June 1943 and typical of her, the first thing she did was to reassure him that his family:

'. . . are all very well and have been exceedingly brave through all this. Nesta's baby is lovely and always talking about 'Uncle Atholl' – I shall be able to tell him a thing or two when he is older! You will be amazed to hear that I am a fully-fledged Doctor now. I qualified in December, unfortunately not in June. But I got Surgery in June so my efforts were not entirely wasted. At the moment I am a House Surgeon at the Municipal Hospital here in Bradford. Life is extremely harassing at times but I enjoy the work very much and have been exceedingly lucky in the chief I have – he has an extraordinary amount of patience! My six months appointment with him finishes in the middle of August and then I shall probably do six months Midwifery. Up to going to press my only achievements in the Surgical line are one amputation and the removal of two Appendices. I was a wreck at the end of each! . . .'

After telling him about Billy who was with the Fleet Air Arm somewhere in America, she continued:

Letter to Atholl's family regarding the *Prisoner of War Journal*.

WAR ORGANISATION JEM/RM.
OF THE
BRITISH RED CROSS SOCIETY and ORDER OF ST. JOHN OF JERUSALEM

President: | *Grand Prior:*
HER MAJESTY THE QUEEN. | H.R.H. The DUKE OF GLOUCESTER, K.G.

PRISONERS OF WAR DEPARTMENT

Chairman:
MAJOR-GENERAL SIR RICHARD HOWARD-VYSE, K.C.M.G., D.S.O.

Deputy Chairman:
J. M. EDDY, C.B.E.

FAR EAST SECTION.
Controller: S. G. KING

TELEPHONE No.:
REGENT 0111 (5 LINES)

9, PARK PLACE,
ST. JAMES'S STREET,
LONDON. S.W.1

When replying please quote reference:

FE/20017.

A. Duncan, Esq.,
Mansfield,
St. Andrews,
Fife.

July 1st, 1943.

Dear Mr. Duncan,

<u>Captain. A. A. Duncan.</u>

Thank you for your letter of the 26th of June.

We would like to say that we notified our Publicity Department on the 11th of this month asking them to send the Prisoner of War Journal monthly, but as you will realise, due to the very great number that have to be published it may not be possible for them to supply you with this particular month, however, we have written to them again asking them to do all they can to send you the June copy.

Yours sincerely,

S. G. KING,

Controller.

'. . . He always asks when he writes if I have heard about you and will be delighted when the good news reaches him. He has spent the last year telling me not to worry as he felt you were alright – but it is not so easy to believe when it is the rest of your life at stake . . . I hope you appreciate the valiant effort I am making with this type-writer as it is my first attempt and rather a slow one too ... anyhow I expect you won't mind much so long as letters arrive after such a long while. You must have longed for news . . .'

In her next letter, dated 18 June, she told him that in January 1943 she had had yet more of her letters returned (which she had posted to him a year earlier) and went on,

'. . . It was rather strange but a few days before we got news of you (May
1943) I had decided to write to you in the hope that it might eventually
reach you – I must be getting psychic . . .'

For the rest of this letter she brought him up-to-date with events over the
preceding year or so, and thanked him again for the beautiful crocodile
handbag that he had sent to her in late 1941(in his letters home that
Christmas he had been worried about the possibility of his mail going down
on one of the many ships which were sunk). Her letter thanking him had
never reached him as it was one of those returned undelivered, so now she
could try again.

She continued to type fortnightly letters and on 7 August wrote to tell
him that Billy had come home on leave unexpectedly and she had taken a
brief holiday with him and their parents. She was looking forward to
returning to work though because,

'hospital life is pleasant – plenty of variety and not so much time to sit and
think as when I am sitting at home doing nothing. The thought of my next
job rather gives me the jitters but then so did the other. The first week or so
is the worst before you get into the routine and it is a little less harassing . . .
It will be wonderful when we do eventually see you again and every day is
one nearer. It is bad enough now but nothing could be worse than that
awful fourteen months when we never heard a word. I thought at times I
would go mad. Bunty found the same as I did that the only thing to do was
work and she has certainly kept very busy helping your father.'

After this letter was sent, restrictions were imposed that limited letters to
just 25 words and for the rest of that year her letter writing was just a frustrating series of staccato phrases.

The first letter from his family was written on 12 June, 1943. It was sent
by Nesta and George, and gave him news of the family and of course, baby
George, now two and a half years old and talking constantly of his 'Uncle
Atholl who is in Japan . . . and a soldier Captain!'

The next one was from Mansefield, dated 3 July, and was written in three
parts starting with his mother who wrote the following:

'. . . it was dreadful waiting for over fourteen long months for news of you,
till one day the blessed telegram arrived from the War Office to give us the
good news that you were alive . . . we receive many enquiries from your
many friends. The latest to enquire personally is Dicky (viz. Atholl's old
school friend, Robert Dickson), who walked in this morning. He is looking
very well, and there is little change in him. His firm is very pleased with his
work, and even admitting that it has a monopoly, he has done well . . .'

This innocent remark hides a coded message which Atholl could interpret easily: the firm Dicky worked for was the RAF and he had been on active service (pre-war he had been stationed in Singapore where he had been on the flying boats). She had circumvented the censorship restrictions to reassure Atholl that Dicky was safe. One month later, writing as though he was still at home in Woodburn Terrace, St Andrews, but in actual fact back again on active service, Dicky wrote to Atholl once again using the same code:

'. . . apart from the official telegram your people have still had no news directly from yourself. I am well, though working at present rather far from home. My firm is tremendously busy of course, having a virtual monopoly in its own line, with strongest competition coming from the Americans, who are doing a lot of exporting. Before I left my previous position I had the satisfaction of knowing that I had done so well in cleaning up the muddle there that there was nothing left for me to tackle, and when I say nothing at all, you know I really mean it, for you know of old how thorough I am once I get my teeth into a problem . . .'

This letter would not reach Atholl until June 1944 when he marked it No. 18. The family letter then goes on to talk about contact with the Red Cross and mail coming to United Kingdom from prisoners in Japan.

'The weather too was on its best behaviour, in fact it has been wonderfully good all this year, after the mildest winter for many years, and it is not surprising that everything in the garden is lovely just now. Baby George is a lovely child, tall for his age; is very intelligent, and is longing to see you, as we are.

I do hope we shall soon be allowed to send you a parcel. Meantime we contribute to the Red Cross regularly in the hope that some of their parcels will reach you, dear. And in the Red Cross *Prisoners of War* magazine, we have been reading a short description of the conditions prevailing in the Far East Prisoner of War camps, including the Fukuoka group. And we heard over the radio that about seven thousand letters and postcards had been received in this country from prisoners in Japanese hands, and that more had since been sent from all the camps except three, for which postal arrangements were not yet complete. So we are hoping to hear from you soon, Atholl, and trusting also that you will soon be receiving communications from us.'

Bunty's paragraph followed her mother's and she sent him news from Uncle Alec and his family, told him of film shows she has been to see, notably the newly released *Mrs Miniver*, in which the male lead was, she thought, the double of her young brother. She finished with the latest news

The Prisoner of War

THE OFFICIAL JOURNAL OF THE PRISONERS OF WAR DEPARTMENT OF THE RED CROSS AND ST. JOHN WAR ORGANISATION, ST. JAMES'S PALACE, LONDON, S.W.I

VOL. 2. No. 13   Free to Next of Kin   MAY, 1943

The Far East   *A Broadcast from Java*

LIFE IN A JAPANESE PRISON CAMP

The canteens are not well stocked, but some sweets and tobacco can be bought. Each man also receives a ration of between 150 and 200 cigarettes monthly.

There are only a few books in the camps; the International Red Cross Committee delegate hopes to supply both books and games. The Japanese have confiscated playing-cards in order to prevent gambling. (*Visited March.*)

FUKUOKA GROUP OF CAMPS

This group of seven camps is administered from **Fukuoka**, in **Kyushu**, the most southerly island of Japan. The names of the camps are **Ube, Omine, Ohama, Motoyama, Higashimisome, Mukojima** and **Innoshima**. They contain British prisoners of war from Hong Kong and Java, and some naval prisoners of war. Two of the camps are on islands in the Inland Sea.

Although fewer details are available about this group of camps, it appears that in many respects they resemble the **Osaka** group. The Japanese have supplied clothing. The food is based on that given to Japanese troops, modified for European tastes, and includes bread and cereals. The prisoners, when not working, study languages, including Japanese, and read books. Work averages eight hours a day. The canteen supplies are limited. The prisoners get five or six cigarettes a day. No mail has yet been received or sent. The International Red Cross Committee delegate has still got a reserve of relief supplies and will send some to these camps. The morale is said to be good. (*Visited March.*)

Further notes on these camps will appear in our next issue.

Extract from front cover of May 1943 edition of *Prisoner of War* magazine mentioning the Fukuoka Group of Camps, one of which they knew Atholl was in.

on baby George. Finally his father added a brief paragraph in which he reiterated how much pleasure they all derived from at last being able to write to him.

The next jointly written letter from the family was dated 20 August. In the first paragraph Bunty informed him about an air crash in Eire involving a civil flying boat from Lisbon in Portugal which had been loaded with Far East mail, and had crashed on Mount Brandon on the Dingle peninsula as it came in to land at Shannon in southern Ireland. Over 27,000 letters and postcards were destroyed in the accident and they were fearful that word from him had been lost in the disaster.

Over 20 years later in 1966 when I was 13, Dad and Mum took us all for a fortnight's holiday to south-west Ireland and we stayed in a hotel in Dingle town. During that holiday Dad set off and climbed part way up Mount Brandon. It is only recently that I have realised the real reason behind this – he wanted to visit the crash site.

This was the last long letter that they would be able to send to him and in it they told him about life in the town, the comings and goings including recent marriages. They passed on best wishes sent from several of his former teachers. One of these was his physics master at Madras, Alfie Law who a year later was to send Atholl a postcard which lifted not only his spirits but also the rest of the camp when it arrived early in 1945. It detailed in code the events which had taken place in Europe during the summer of 1944, having got through all the censors. Atholl would be the only person in the camp who could have deciphered it. Desperate times and circumstances led to such ingenuity, and the smallest pieces of card could bring unimaginable hope. Such is the power of the written word.

Another teacher who sent greetings was Professor Edgar Dickie, Dean of St Mary's College at the university. The professor had already penned a card to Atholl on 28 June in which he said he hoped to be able to send him books on behalf of the university through a scheme he had launched in 1940 for the benefit of British prisoners in Europe. This card would take almost a year to reach Atholl and it would be marked No. 2, the second item of mail that he received in captivity.

Elizabeth's next letter was written on 5 July. She was in reminiscent mood:

'. . . Just lately I have been thinking such a lot about the grand times we used to have in St Andrews. I did a mighty small amount of work in those days considering what I should have done and at the time I used to get very worried, as no doubt you will remember but I don't regret one moment of it and I am only too thankful we had the sense to enjoy ourselves while we had the opportunity.'

She told him about the antics of several of her patients and went on to mention other members of the medical staff:

'By the way one of the residents at St Luke's comes from Dunfermline and his father is in the same trade as yours. His name is McCulloch and he says his father often goes to St A. He did Medicine at Edinburgh for which I duly sympathise from time to time much to his anger! He had two brothers but unfortunately one died from malaria in Africa a few weeks ago.

The husband of a friend of ours in Bradford has recently been notified as being a Prisoner in your part of the world – he was also in Java. His name is Heap incidentally – you never know, you may come across him, funny things like that do happen.'

Despite it being nearly a year before these letters would reach him, the first to do so was one of Elizabeth's, dated 15 July 1943 and the fourth letter she wrote to him that summer.

In Japan, just a week after she had written that letter, without warning he and several other British officers were transferred to another camp. He had received no mail while in the camp in Java or during the time he was at Motoyama. He still had a long wait.

These letters that Elizabeth and his family were sending to 'Fukuoka Camps' would arrive at Zentsuji, the officers' camp and his new 'home' on Shikoku Island, in March 1944 almost a year after he had been transferred there. But he was lucky. Many prisoners of war didn't receive a single letter

Medical staff at
St Luke's Hospital,
Bradford:
seated, left to right –
Dr Bruce McCulloch,
Resident Surgical
Officer, Dr Douglas,
Medical Superintenent,
Dr Elizabeth Glassey,
Senior House Officer.
Standing far left and far
right are two American
surgeons who were
seconded to the staff at
St Luke's for several
months.

or postcard, let alone a cable, throughout the duration of their captivity. He was in so many ways very lucky, and he knew it.

It was in early October that an official War Office communiqué, dated 30 September 1943, notified his family that Captain A. A. Duncan had been transferred to 'ZENTSUJI Camp'.

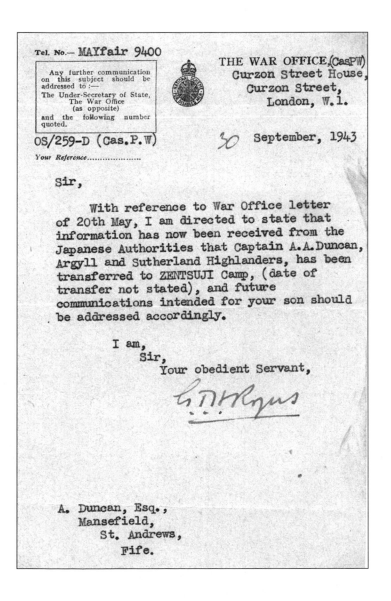

Official notification of Atholl's transfer to Zentsuji Camp – September 1943.

Captain Duncan's Japanese Prison Camp Record Card. (Reproduced by kind permission of the Public Record Office, Kew: PRO document ref. no. WO345/15.)

整理番號	3011

收容所 Camp	廣島 福岡 善通寺 爪哇 20. 8. 13. 昭17年 8月 15日	番 號 No.	福岡 爪本 善本443 善本667
姓 名 Name	Duncan, Andrew Atholl ダンカン, アンドルゥ, アソール.	生年月日 Date of Birth	1918. 3. 4
國 籍 Nationality	英	所屬部隊 Unit	No. 100911 Argyll & Sutherland Highlanders
階級身分 Rank	Captain 陸軍大尉 A. CAPT		
捕獲場所 Place of Capture	爪哇	捕獲年月日 Date of Capture	昭和 17年 3月 8日
父ノ名 Father's Name	Duncan Andrew	母ノ名 Mother's Name	Duncan Emelia
本籍地 Place of Origin	Mansfield St. Andrews Fifeshire. Scotland	職 業 Occupation	學生.
通報先 Destination of Report	Andrew Duncan Mansfield. St Andrews, Fifeshire, Scotland	特記事項 Remark	

Chapter 9

First Christmas in Zentsuji

July–December 1943

The diary picks up the story of their arrival, on 29 July 1943, at the Officers' Camp at Zentsuji, after the overnight journey from Motoyama:

> . . . we hired a bullock cart for the baggage and after about a mile's hike reached our new home which was an old army barracks where the German prisoners in the last war had been housed during their stay in Japan, and where there were already quite a few American, Australian and British prisoners, of all services. There were Yanks from Guam, Wake and Philippines, Aussies from Rabaul and district and British from the 'Exeter' and other ships which had been sunk in the Java Sea actions. Once again our kits were searched and such articles as drugs, knives and books and my flying goggles were confiscated, tho' we were told that the books would be put into the library for the benefit of all. After that we had to sign the usual document about escape and were then allowed to go to our room. Our quarters (Room 8B) consisted of a fairly large room about 50' × 25' with a central passage separating four wood platforms covered with matting, each platform being capable of accommodating seven people or eight with a crush. Above each platform at the back was a single shelf about 18" wide to take our gear, whilst each side of the room had a table with two forms: three blankets and a pillow, two bowls and a cup, fork and spoon completed the issues made to us. As the whole construction was made of wood and was old bed bugs abounded and after lights out these pests along with fleas made life a misery for us. For the first few days we were not allowed out of our quarters except for toilet purposes as we were in quarantine but after being 'glass-rodded' we were given a clean bill of health and moved to another room (Room 18) in the other block and officially came on the strength.
>
> After a short speech by the Col. i/c who told us that there were no idlers in Japan and that we would be required to volunteer for work – agriculture, rabbits or chickens – we were allotted our various duties and settled down to the usual humdrum existence of a prison camp. Although there was not so much food as in our last camp it was far better cooked and the inclusion of beans in the rice helped matters greatly. Also bread was issued for lunch and

we got a small amount of milk about once every ten days, tho' the issues of the latter two ceased not long after our arrival. There was a canteen in the camp but this had long ceased to operate except for the occasional sale of vitamin pills and tea and the canteen hut was used for the concerts and church services every Sunday, the former being excellent entertainment despite the ban on musical instruments and dressing up.

This drawing of inside Room 18, Zentsuji Officers Camp, was drawn by Captain Duncan in 1943. The view is from his bunk.

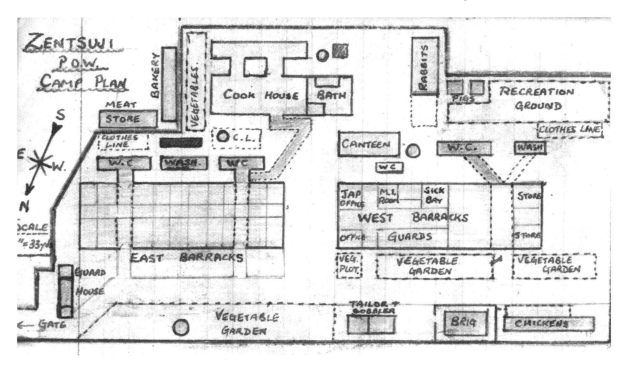

Plan of Zentsuji Prisoner of War Camp, drawn by Captain Duncan in 1943.

By an extraordinary coincidence, in July 1943 (the same month as he was transferred to Zentsuji) the American National Red Cross (ANRC) published an article and photograph of the camp on the front page of their monthly magazine for families of prisoners of war. At that time Atholl's family only knew that he was being held 'somewhere in Japan in one of the Fukuoka Camps'. The family received a copy (whether it came direct from the ANRC or from Alec Rattray is not recorded), but either way I am sure it will have been thanks to Alec that they had it.

The article reproduced on p. 159 describes conditions at the camp vividly. The photograph is interesting as the men had signed their names on it; sitting centre front is Lieutenant Payne, US Army Air Corps, who was mentioned in the diary following a lecture he gave about the situation in China in early October.

The report ends '. . . a comparison with reports which have been received on other Japanese camps suggests that Zentsuji is probably among the best.'

Atholl would have agreed with this last statement for not only in the next extract from his diary, but also for the rest of his life, he attributed his survival largely to having been transferred to Zentsuji and spending the longest time of his captivity in these 'more favourable' conditions. His diary continues:

Our party of 30 . . . was the first of five to arrive and for the next few days parties came in, bringing the total of new arrivals – all officers – to 300 and when we had all got settled down, an issue of an American Red X parcel and a CCC (housewife kit) was made, the only snag being that all meats fish and soup were extracted and sent over to the cookhouse or galley, to be issued when it was considered necessary to augment our rations. When we came into camp, the people already in residence gave us a wonderful reception and if any of us were deficient in clothing, soap or any other small article it was produced – no payment being accepted. There was a wonderful spirit of cama-raderie which I had not met in any other camp. Probably what I appreciated most of all was to hear other peoples' experiences and from what I can make out we seemed to have got off very lightly all along the line with the exception of the 'Singapore Maru' episode. Some of the stories are worth putting down and so here are a few of them:

When the American and Filipino forces on Bataan capitulated they were stripped of all their possessions and kit by the Japanese and although these men had been starving for about a month, were divided into groups of 500–1,000 and forced to march the 120 odd kilometres from Mariveles to San Fernando, the first day 57 km being covered with only one ten minute halt and no water being provided. The whole march was completed in four days and stragglers and sick – suffering from malaria and dysentry – were shot and bayoneted, some being put to death while their friends were helping them along. The Japs were bringing heavy artillery down the road while the Americans were moving up and the heavy artillery opened up from Corrige-dor on this (Japanese artillery), killing many of their own men. Several of the senior officers committed suicide while others were bayoneted . . . anyone in possession of Jap money shot out of hand . . . there were cases of Filipino troops being buried alive and left to die a miserable death. The conditions when they got into camp were no better and at one time, the sick were dying too quickly for the burial squads to cope with the numbers, and although several attempts at escape were made, they all ended in tragedy the Japs dividing the prisoners up into groups of ten so that if one of the ten tried to escape, the remaining nine would be shot. This was put into effect on more than one occasion.

Opposite:
Front cover of *American Red Cross Bulletin* showing picture of American officers at Zentsuji Prisoner of War Camp. Lieutenant Payne USAC marked by arrow.

PRISONERS OF WAR BULLETIN

Published by the American National Red Cross for the Relatives of American Prisoners of War and Civilian Internees

VOL. 1, NO. 2   WASHINGTON, D. C.   JULY 1943

Prisoner of War Camps in Japan—Zentsuji

By John Cotton

The camp of Zentsuji was opened on January 16, 1942, and is situated in the northern part of the large island of Shikoku, four miles from Tadotsu near the Inland Sea. It comprises six acres of a fertile plain between two hills covered with pines. The climate is good, and there are no diseases endemic to the neighborhood. The first report from an International Red Cross Committee Delegate who visited the camp stated that the men were at work clearing a nearby hill for planting potatoes, vegetables, and wheat, and that they were paid for this work; while others, working within the camp on necessary upkeep, were being paid somewhat less. The latest report received shows that there were 234 American prisoners (including 54 officers), and 62 Australian officers, in a total camp population of 320.

The buildings comprise two Army barracks two stories high, well ventilated, with the kitchen in a separate building. The barracks have recently been divided into rooms containing from one to fourteen camp beds, each having five thin blankets, a pillow, and a counterpane. Officers have mattresses in addition. Heat is supplied by what are described as "modern stoves." Sanitation facilities were reported to be clean and sufficiently distant from the main buildings. Hot baths are permitted once a week, or twice a week for laborers; cold showers are available every day.

Improvement in Clothing and Rations

Clothing at the camp was reported to be insufficient at first, but later reports indicate that captured uniforms and overcoats had been sup-

plied to prisoners, and that these were sufficient for cold weather.

The daily food ration is reported to be 300 grams (10½ oz.) of bread; 300 grams (10½ oz.) of rice; 160 grams (5½ oz.) of wheat; plus potatoes, vegetables, fish, and eggs. Working prisoners in divisional labor camps are given some extra food. The average weight of the men in one working party was reported to be around 144 lbs. on March 9, 1943—after about a year of captivity.

Some of the working parties going out from this camp are tilling the soil, loading and unloading goods at neighboring railway stations, and

laboring in a village bakery. Within the camp the prisoners are raising rabbits to supplement their rations and at last reports there were over 200.

There is an infirmary in the camp and a military hospital nearby. One Japanese doctor is permanently attached to the camp and is assisted by three prisoner doctors. There is a monthly medical inspection of all prisoners.

Sports space is provided for baseball, cricket, and deck tennis, with a "gymnastic excursion" outside the camp once a week. Radio is available, for local reception, and a library of some 500 books was obtained from

American prisoners of war at Zentsuji. This group includes five aviators from the U. S. S. Houston

A week or two later he notes in his diary that,

> *. . . it is the custom in this country not to punish individuals but the group, this having been the case right from the start of the feudal system and holds good not only for the army but the civilians; another point in this connection being that there is not such a thing as privacy in Japan, as the Japs believe that this is a bad thing.*
>
> *. . . In Singapore, itself, after the surrender many Chinese were seized by the Japs roped together in parties of 10 and either bayoneted or dumped into the sea. One of these managed to escape and hid in Changi POW camp where he worked in the cookhouse.*

It is small wonder that the prisoners constantly feared for their lives when so many of them could relate such appalling first-hand accounts of Japanese excesses. However, despite this, it seems they took every opportunity to get one over on the Japs as the following accounts reveal:

> *. . . there was a great demand for petrol after the surrender, the Chinese paying very high prices for this, and many varied schemes were employed to obtain it. One lovely story concerns one of our men who was i/c of a steam roller being used in repair work. This individual used to apply for, and draw, $1\frac{1}{2}$ galls of petrol daily to operate his steam roller!!!*
>
> *. . . When our men were required to construct a shrine to commemorate the Japanese war dead, they urinated in the concrete when it was being mixed and used to collect white ants in tins out at Changi and release these when working on the shrine, with the result that the concrete crumbled easily and the white ants started to eat away the woodwork . . .*

Thankfully books were now in plentiful supply and very soon classes and lessons started up again.

> *There is a good library in camp, most of the books having been supplied by the American embassy and as there are quite a large number of textbooks in it, classes have been started in a great many varying subjects; I started off by attending the physical chem. and calculus classes but found it impossible to concentrate and had to give it up. I hope that this mental torpor I have developed is not going to continue after I get out of here, and I have been con-*

siderably worried as to what I am going to do after the war is over . . . the other night I had a very vivid dream about my getting married and my feelings upon waking and finding myself still a prisoner in the hands of these god-forsaken rats can well be imagined!

Not long after we had been in this camp, a grand re-shuffle of rooms took place and in our own room (no18) we have a Dutch room commander (Capt. Oyens of the DEI Air Force) the remainder being American Navy, Army and Air force, with British Navy and Army as well, one Australian being the sole representative of that country . . . Old Mac has joined the band of super-optimists and is firmly convinced that there is a good chance of the whole show being over by the new year – arguing that events happening at the present time show a distinct similarity to 1918, and no less a person than Capt. Gordon, RN, late of HMS 'Exeter' is also my confidant about an early release; of course they are assuming that Japan will pack in along with Germany, but somehow I feel that they will continue to fight for a short while at least: however, time will tell.

Quite a few of the Americans in the camp have received mail from home and whenever the post comes along we always eagerly ask, 'Is there any for the British?' but so far we have been out of luck. To see other people getting news from home always makes me feel homesick and is very depressing but with any luck there should be something for me in the near future.

On the afternoon of September 10th we were sitting on our beds reading and awaiting the arrival of the meal, when suddenly the whole building started to tremble just as if some giant had seized one end of it and was trying to see-saw it out of the ground. The windows rattled fiercely and the uprights (wood) creaked and groaned ominously when just as suddenly as it had started the tremor passed. Although we had several more shocks during the next few days none was as bad as the initial one and we were very pleased to read in the newspapers a few days later that considerable damage had been done at Tottori about 400 deaths having occurred and over 5,000 houses demolished. It would be damned hard luck to have come through everything so far and then be killed in an earthquake. Another thought that occurred to me at the time was that if they had another 'quake similar to that which they had in 1923 they would have to pack in right away which is rather a pleasing thought . . .

On Sept 23rd a party from the chicken squad went down to the coast to collect some sand for the hens – a total distance of ten miles – and I was lucky enough to be in their number. Going down to the coast was quite easy but coming back that damned sand seemed to get heavier and heavier so that by the time we got back to camp most of us were all-in but after a good meal – we got about twice our normal ration both at lunch and supper due to Twiss' wanglings (Lt. Frank Twiss RN, late of HMS *Exeter* and head of the

Lieutenant Frank Twiss
RN, late of HMS *Exeter*.

'chicken squad') – and a shower, I felt as fit as a fiddle. Its good to know that I still do have a little strength left. The weather has changed all of a sudden and quite frequently of late I have found it necessary to wear my battledress to keep warm and the Nips have issued us with great coats (captured British coats from Hong Kong) but will not allow us to wear them; a typical Nip gesture. Well, that now brings my diary up to date so from now onward I hope to make daily entries to keep track of events as they take place.

His entries for the rest of September relate to settling into the camp routine and a preoccupation with the topic of food: the irritation of noisy eaters, obsessively watching as food was served, the discomfort of severe indigestion (for which the doctors among their number were unable to help) and joining the 'chicken squad'. He resumes his reviews of the 'Dailies', the *Osaka Mainichi* and the *Nippon Times* (propaganda newspapers), cutting out and keeping articles of note or interest and having discussions with room mates on the progress of the war.

On Sunday 26th he writes:

Today being Sunday we are allowed to lie on our bunks all day long if we so desire, and is the only day of the week on which this privilege is granted. The morning was spent, completing a pair of mittens I made from an odd scrap of blanket material; in preparation for the forthcoming winter and then toffing myself up for the church service at 10.15am. I try to make myself as presentable as possible each Sunday as it helps to bring back a feeling of self respect so dig out the old Sam Browne and don a clean rig out and then sally forth. I was talking to Tom Magee the other day – he comes from San Francisco – and in the course of the conversation mentioned Alec Rattray; much to my surprise, Tom seemed to know him so I have asked him to look him up when we get out of here. At the same time Tom let us read a letter that he had got from Mary Astor the film star, and it turned out that he knew her very well. It was a very amusing and cheery letter but what really did tickle my fancy was the cancellation mark of the stamp which read, 'The marines are coming'. Let's hope that they are not too long about it for I feel that I have overstayed my welcome in the land of the cherry blossoms (and benjo) . . . afternoon was spent discussing the exchange of various articles from our respective countries with some of the Americans, most of them being particularly keen to try some of our Scottish foods and drinks.

Opposite:
Record of proposed
exchange of goods
listed in one of his
notebooks.

K.G. SCHACHT. (BUCK)
1ST EXCHANGE.
FOOD HAMPER UP TO £3-0-0 INCLUDING :—
CURRANT BUN, DUNDEE CAKE, SHORT BREAD,
HAGGIS, OATCAKES, BUTTERSCOTCH, WOODS WINE
BISCUITS, DIGESTIVE BISCUITS, MARZIPAN WALNUTS
EDINBURGH ROCK. AND SPECIAL XMAS PLUM PUD.
YOUMA BREAD. TERRY'S COFFEE CHOCOLATE.
ALSO DESIRES HARRIS TWEED JACKET, SKEAN
DHU. CAP BADGES, SHETLAND SHAWL, FAIR ISLE
PULLOVER. GOLF CLUBS. ATHOLL BROSE

WILL SEND :—
WAFFLE IRON, PEACHES, APPLES, PEANUT BUTTER
AIR PHOTOS. SUBMARINE INSIGNIA, SILEX
COFFEE MAKER.
IF FOOD STILL RATIONED, WILL RUSH FOOD PARCEL
CONSISTING OF :—
SUGAR 7lbs, BULLY 12 TINS, BUTTER 7lbs
TEA 3lbs, COFFEE 3lbs, CHEESE ASMT. 5lbs
CHOCOLATE 3lbs, HAM 3lbs, DRIED FRUITS 7lbs
COCOA 3lbs. LIMIT. 50lbs AND/OR $25.00
CABLE :— SEND BOX ———— IF REQUIRED

WARREN STIRLING. 1ST EXCHANGE.
ATHOLL BROSE AND GENERAL FOOD HAMPER.
RECIPE BOOKS.
WILL SEND :— BABY CYCLONE ENGINE
AND AIR PHOTOGRAPHS.

GEORGE H. ARMSTRONG.
1ST EXCHANGE.

GENERAL FOOD HAMPER. CRAIG TARTAN
TRAVELLING RUG, FAIRISLE PULLOVER, SKEAN
DHU, HEATHER MIXTURE HARRIS, SCONE
RECIPE. ENGLISH CIGARETTES. ATHOLLBROSE.

WILL SEND. :—
AIR PHOTOS, INSIGNIA, RECIPE BOOKS AND RECIPES
BLACK WALNUTS, PECANS, AMERICAN CHEESE
ASSORTMENT, COOKIE, CANDY, + CAKE SAMPLER,
BOSTON BROWN BREAD, PRALINES, APPLETS,
POPCORN, FRITOS, [FOOD PARCEL, IF REQUIRED,
IN CASE OF RATIONING]
IF DUTY ON HARRIS TWEED IS LESS IN
CANADA THAN IN U.S.A., SEND SUCH ITEMS
TO GEORGE c/o. R.H. BROWN, KELOWNA,
B.C. CANADA.
BALSA WOOD, AIR MAGAZINES,

JAMES H. BALDWIN. 1ST EXCHANGE.

WILL WRITE FOR SCOTTISH FOODS AND CABLE
BANK DRAFT.

CAN SUPPLY :— STAMPS, PIÑA CLOTH, CARVED
WOOD SETS, CIGARS. WILL FORWARD DETAILS OF
PRICES ETC.

M.C. (RHEEN) TUYN.
1ST EXCHANGE.
FOOD HAMPER INCLUDING. CURRANT BUN, HAGGIS
WOODS WINE BISCUITS, MARZIPAN WALNUTS, EDINBURGH ROCK,
DUNDEE CAKE, CARLTON PUDDING, PLUM PUDDING, OXFORD
MARMALADE.

WILL SEND :—
COFFEE, TEA STAMPS

LEE C. BROOKS.
1ST EXCHANGE.
SEND UP TO £3-0-0. FOOD HAMPER CONTAINING :—
CURRANT BUN, DUNDEE CAKE, WOODS WINE BISCUITS,
MARZIPAN WALNUTS, DIGESTIVE BISCUITS, OXFORD & KEILLER
MARMALADE, YOUMA BREAD, EDINBURGH ROCK. HAGGIS.

WILL SEND. :—
MAPLE SYRUP, FIG NEWTONS, GRAHAM CRACKERS,
CAMMEMBERT CHEESE, PRESERVED FRUITS, BOUND
COPIES OF "LIFE".

ERWIN W. LASHER.
1ST EXCHANGE.
DESIRES :— TWEEDS.

WILL SEND. :—
PIÑA CLOTH TABLE SETS, MANILLA CIGARS IN CABINET.
HARDWOOD CARVED CRUET AND SALAD BOWL.

DAVID HUTCHINSON-SMITH.

WANTS :— TWEEDS, TARTAN CLOTH, SCOTTISH FOODS,
DEVON CREAM CHOCOLATE, CAP BADGE.

WILL SUPPLY :— FOOD HAMPER, TINNED GOODS, KANGAROO HIDE GOODS.
STAMPS.

ANGUS M. MORRIS.
WISHES. HAGGIS AND INFORMATION ABOUT TWEEDS.
WILL EXCHANGE MAPLE SYRUP FOR HAGGIS.

Throughout October, entries dealt with incidents that occurred as well as the monotony of life in general. He refers to some of the Japs by nicknames, such as the Kendo Kid (Jap supply sergeant), Sake Pete, Pluto San and Joe Cambridge (Asabuki). Shiro Asabuki was the camp interpreter and so named because he had studied at Trinity College, Cambridge, from 1935 to 1938. In 1997 when Dad recalled this man, he remembered him as quite a reasonable type of Nip; if he could help within limits he would, for instance getting hold of paper and writing materials. He came from a very good family background and was wearing civvies when Dad had first met him. Later on he disappeared for a week and reappeared with his head shaved and in Jap uniform and when the prisoners of war cheered him, he just nodded politely. Eventually he was posted elsewhere and there was a new interpreter who, continuing the 'Disney' theme, went by the nickname, Donald Duck.

October entries included more first-hand accounts of incidents and sea battles. Not so surprising really as for some of the prisoners of war, Dad included, these personal accounts must have been the life-blood of conversations in camp; they had individually and collectively experienced so much, what else could these men talk about with such authority? And after all, de-briefing is a fundamental part of military life. He wrote out an eye-witness account of the sinking of the POW ship the *Lisbon Maru* which was given at a lecture on 4th October:

Lieut Bucke, RC Sigs gave us the facts about the 'Lisbon Maru' this evening and here is a summary of his story. After the fall of Hong Kong on Dec 25th 1941, the prisoners were taken to the mainland and imprisoned. After a short time, the Japs separated the officers from the men as too many escapes had been attempted and up till Sept 18th patchy communications were maintained between the two camps notes occasionally being sent inside bread rolls which were baked in one camp. On the officers being brought back to the main camp they found appalling conditions with all men suffering from some form of malnutrition, beriberi, scurvy, pellagra, dysentery and diphtheria having taken a heavy toll. Three large huts which had been canteens were now used as 'lying-in' mortuaries. One man when he died weighed only 38lbs. The officers on arrival were told that they had to select 2,000 men fit to travel overseas but the most they could raise was 1817 who embarked on 25th Sept on the 'Lisbon Maru' – an old Glen Line boat of about 6–7,000 tons – the POW being accommodated in the three forward holds as shown in sketch.

Before sailing two men were taken ashore as they had diphtheria and dysentery. On 27th Sept the ship sailed hugging the China coast till Oct 1st, Lt. Col. Stuart of the Middlesex Regt being i/c POW. At 7.10am on the 1st,

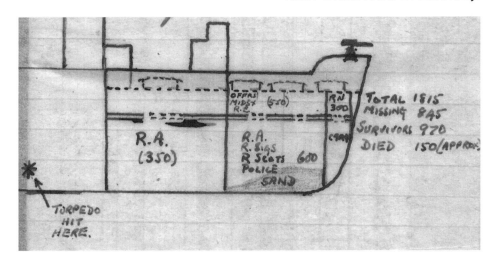

Sketch in the diary shows distribution of prisoners of war on board *Lisbon Maru*.

just before roll call a torpedo hit the boat amidships. There were about 1,000 Jap troops on board who had been accommodated in the aft holds, and these charged about in a panic. The prow and stern guns began firing at random not knowing where to aim. All POW were kept below and the sick and galley staff were sent down below as well. Then the latrines and wooden companion ways down to the holds were removed. After being hit the engines stopped and the ship lost way. No breakfast was forthcoming to the prisoners and although repeated attempts were made to get in touch with the interpreter, the sentries who had been posted at the hatch would not go for him. In the afternoon other shipping came on the scene and all the Japs bar three were transferred to other ships after the hatches had been boarded over and tarpaulins lashed down over the boards excluding light and ventilation, the ships lighting growing dimmer and then failing. As there were dysentry cases on board and no latrines in the holds, containers had to be used and in the darkness, these were often accidentally knocked over the people in the lower part of the hold. In spite of this, the morale of the troops was good.

After a while water could be heard in the aft forward hold and late that night Lt. Hilton who was in that hold managed to communicate thro' the bulkhead with the main hold and said that they too were lashed down, water was gaining in the hold altho' they had been hand pumping all day and that 75% of the men were unconscious due to lack of oxygen and the remainder were in a very bad shape. That night the vessel was got under tow but progress was very slow and it was apparent that the vessel was slowly sinking. During the night one of the Royal Scots in the main hold managed to prise free one of the boards over the hatch and, the other holds on being told of this, did the same. Next morning about 7 o'clock the vessel listed badly so Col. Stuart ordered a break to be made. A razor blade was produced, the tarpaulin and lashing were cut and five men scrambled through on to the deck and were immediately fired upon by three sentries who were posted in the bow, bridge and bridge roof but none was hit. They immediately took cover and managed to get back into the hold after freeing the other holds with the information that some islands were in sight about 5–6 miles away and that five or six ships were lying between them and the land. Unfortunately one man was shot and killed getting back into the hold. On hearing this, a rush was made for the hatch which caused the ship to list sharply so that water came over the side and into the hold but the ship slowly righted itself and order was restored and life belts issued to everyone.

Hilton then reported all was OK as the stern was on the bottom so parties proceeded on deck but were not fired on by either sentries or other ships who had opened MG fire on the hatches when the first party left the hold; most of the men could not be persuaded to take to the water but some did and swam towards the other ships only to discover that they could not get on board as altho' the rails were lined with Jap troops who dangled lines into the water, the ropes were drawn up out of the water whenever any of our men tried to grab them so there was nothing for it but to make for the land. Later, about 11am the other boats did pick up survivors when the 'Lisbon Maru' had finally sunk, but no Jap troops took any part in the rescue. Unfortunately, the islands nearby did not have any beaches but had low rocky cliffs and very strong tides swept between them, so quite a few of the survivors were smashed against the rocks and killed or swept out to sea to die a lingering death. As regards the Jap sentries who had been left on board the 'Lisbon Maru' one was caught and summarily dealt with. There was practically no food on the rescue ship and survivors were fed on three biscuits and a gill of soya milk twice daily on the journey to Shanghai which was reached on 6th Oct. Many of the men had only a shirt and some were completely naked but nevertheless they were landed on the wharf in this condition. A total of 970 had been saved and of these 35 had to be taken straight to hospital and it wasn't till 5pm on the 6th that they received their first meal since the evening of Sept 30th.

Having recorded these accounts he continued to gather information and on another day writes,

. . . I spent part of the day collecting information about various aspects of the Java campaign and intend to get the full story in the three phases, land, sea and air by the time I have finished. It is amazing just how little I do know about it despite the fact that I was on HQ but then, information was one of our biggest wants at HQ in those days.

Rumours circulated constantly and whenever possible information was elicited from other prisoners of war in the area as the following extracts show:

Joe Kwiatkowski has just come in with the rumour that Hokkaido was bombed by 30 planes yesterday so that, if true, probably accounts for the minor hate session yesterday and today . . .

. . . they often work on unloading wagons from the rail ferry between that port and Kobe and a party of Royal Scots in the latter place doing the same job exchange news with our men by chalking messages on the sides of the trucks! . . .

But frustration was always close to the surface and thoughts of home appear without warning:

Oh God, when is this bloody war going to come to an end? Have been feeling very tired and fed up all day and despite the fact that the news in the papers is good, both the Huns and the Jap withdrawing from various positions, – of course, according to plan! – and Burma has been invaded, I have been feeling pretty depressed; I suppose that it is only natural that one should get such fits under the circumstances in which we live – or should I say, exist – but it makes me mad to think of all the time that I have been forced to waste, time from the best part of my life, and all this due to the incompetence of those in 'high places'; unfortunately, they never are the ones to suffer.

. . . wrote out the draft of a postcard to the folks at home and handed it in for typing. I have just come back from the usual Sunday evening concert which was quite amusing, and faint strains of classical music are drifting into the room from a gramophone recital further down the corridor, bringing a flood of memories of better times back to my mind. How I long for the presence of those so near and dear to me; to be able to sit in comfortable surroundings and see and hear the folks at home but for the present I shall have to be content with memories and daydreams. I wonder how much things will have changed by the time I get back and it is hard to think that most of the people I used to know will be scattered to the four winds or dead, and I shall be practically a stranger in my home town. Still, I suppose that is life . . .

And life was at times very uncomfortable, especially when he was '. . . bothered quite a lot at night by various insects such as bed-bugs and fleas which get inside the blankets and make life a misery . . .'

Such were the problems of communal living despite making every effort himself to eradicate the problem: '. . . have been able to get my clothes boiled out . . . ended up by having to do it surreptitiously and then only getting half of them done the remainder to be dealt with on Saturday . . .'

However, not all irritants could be boiled out:

> . . . the rats which abound in and about the buildings are a positive menace as they scramble all over the shelves during the night, eating whatever they can, having a passion for Wakamoto tablets (sic), and if anyone leaves even a corked bottle lying about, they will eat thro' the cork and then roll the bottle around and so get at the tablets as they fall out.

Despite all the discomforts the prisoners did their best to distract themselves and there are frequent references to music evenings around the gramophone, concerts, shows and recitals. Humour and music were essential ingredients and at Zentsuji there were many who could provide both. It was home to the 'Bath House Gang', a musical ensemble which featured in this mid-October diary entry: '. . . an excellent Hawaiian concert was given tonight, the Bath House Gang providing the music whilst Twiss and Hutch-Smith did a drunken sailor act which nearly brought the house down. What a pair they make!'

The preoccupation with food continued, as the following extracts during that autumn show:

> . . . the Japs decided to rifle the RC parcels and are reputed to have extracted the bully, raisins, prunes, sugar and cheese saying that the last three were unfit for human consumption. Even if this is the case, why do these swine hold up the issue of parcels? . . .
>
> . . . entire supply of raisins, which were abstracted from the RC parcels, have been dumped in the chicken house for distribution to the hens but as about 50% of these could be consumed, an attempt is being made to get them cooked up in the galley. It certainly does hurt to have to throw away such a large quantity of good food.
>
> . . . the food of late has been deplorable, daikon (a type of radish) tops featuring quite regularly on the menu, their presence causing a fair amount of 'bitching' and dismay in the camp in general... RC parcels were dished out last night, and despite the fact that cheese, raisins, prunes and bully had been

removed and in many cases, the sugar, chocolate and hard tack were spoiled by damp and weevils, were very good packages.

. . . in addition to our normal ration of rice we received an issue of 'Kring' (burnt-on rice scraped from the sides of the pans) and as Jackson does not like this, he gave me his portion which I duly ate – but today there was the reckoning in the form of a dose of squitters.

Events during the next couple of weeks were to play a significant part in alleviating fears back home, thanks to Atholl's friendship with an American airman, Lieutenant George Armstrong, USAC.

Oct 20th   *George Armstrong and I were on chicken feeding detail again today and when we were down at the coops George successfully tried to hypnotise some of the hens with most amusing results as the bird would slowly keel over and go to sleep. George is a grand chap – he was a fighter pilot from No. 17 Squadron USAC flying P-40s. He's about 6' 3" tall and has a big chubby face and a delightful slow drawl and can, on occasion, give wonderful imitations of Walt Disney creations much to my delight: his demonstration of Goofy learning to ride a horse is something not to be missed.*

Oct 23rd   *. . . good deal of poker is being played in camp these days . . . thank God that it is only stage money we are playing for as the only use we can put it to here is poker as it is impossible to spend it all even through the canteen and it certainly will be worthless when this war is over. The 6.10am roll call is quite a chilly affair these days as the sun has not risen at that time, and altho' we have been issued with greatcoats and despite the fact that the sentries are wearing theirs, we are not allowed to put ours on – simply because the official Japanese winter season does not commence till Nov 1st!*

Oct 24th–25th   *. . . present moment I am seated at the table writing up the day's news, a bridge quartet are holding post-mortems, on one side of me, old Crossley is snoring peacefully on his bunk behind me, whilst on the other side a group is re-fighting old battles and indulging in recriminations against everyone except themselves, and I am wishing that this war were over and done with as I am heartily sick of being a POW . . .*

Oct 26th   *Two of the Americans in the camp were having an argument today and the conversation took a rather personal turn ending up with one replying to a sally by the other with, 'Well, if I had a dog with a face like yours, I'd shave its arse and make it walk backwards!!!' This morning I discovered that my assets as far as cigarettes were concerned were absolutely nil, and was at my wits' end as to how to procure a smoke when my guardian*

Lieutenant George H. Armstrong, USAC; propaganda photograph taken in Zentsuji Prisoner of War Officers' Camp, 1943.

angel in the form of W/Cmdr Mathews turned up and gave me sufficient to tide me over till the next issue. We were all very pleased to observe the arrival of some more Red Cross supplies in camp today, these being bulk issues of cocoa, sugar, salt and tinned foods and wonder how long it will be before these are issued to us. The American Navy are holding their weekly lecture in our room this evening, Jack Ryder continuing his lecture on submarines . . . Wray and Lazzarini our two salesmen, have been at me trying to obtain one of the tins of porridge oats I possess . . . I have not the slightest intention of parting with this.

Oct 27th   *This morning the chicken squad were called upon to dig up the beds of sweet potatoes opposite the chicken pens and although the yield was very small we did get some entertainment out of despatching three rats and obtaining a near miss on a fourth. I pulled down my flea bag (sleeping bag) today and intend to use the middle layer to make a pullover and balaclava helmet for the winter. The American officers in our half of the room are continually poking fun at some of my pronunciations and jokingly refer to me as 'that Scotchman' knowing that I will certainly take them to task about the Scots and Scotch!* . . . [On the subject of pronunciation, it was after his arrival at Zentsuji that Atholl also became known as 'Andy', his other name. He told me that the reason for this was that some of the Americans with whom he was now sharing life would pronounce his name 'Ath – hole' in such a way that it closely resembled a part of his anatomy being described by someone with a lisp!]

Oct 28th   *. . . six people have been detailed to pack their kits and be ready for a permanent move from this camp after lunch tomorrow. Unfortunately for the community as a whole George Williams, our live-wire concert organiser, is among the six and we are all very sorry to see him go. The Japs have issued each of them with a RC parcel complete, and a large tin of jam as well as soap, towel, boots, handkerchiefs, underwear, and other articles and they are taking a few thousand yen along with them to their new abode to help out their new comrades in that line. This evening a farewell was given in their honour and after it was over a sing-song was held which nearly raised the roof off the building . . . the Japs will not tell them where or why they are leaving but as each of them has had connection with either the press or broadcasting, it is surmised that propaganda may be at the back of it all.*

Oct 29th   *. . . tonight our room has challenged room 17 to charades and we are expecting to have a hilarious evening as . . . most of the younger set in our room all agree that what No. 18 requires is a good rowdy evening to waken it up a bit.*

Oct 30th   *Well, last night we certainly had a rowdy evening and although we lost the contest I have not spent such an enjoyable evening for many a long day . . . tonight we issued a challenge to Pat Brougham's room (22) and for this made arrangements to have a cheer leader so that whenever our side required some encouragement, the necessary was soon forthcoming. On one occasion when I had been exhorted to, 'Come on An...........dy!!' the opposition waited until I had acknowledged the cheer and then started a counter cry of 'Horse shit.' However, victory was ours . . .*

Lieutenant Patrick Brougham, RN, late HMS *Exeter* – a fellow prisoner at Zentsuji Officers' Camp.

Oct 31st   Today we got our first 'hot' bath, being rationed to half a bucket per person but this did not matter too much as we were able to get a cold shower as well, but once the cold weather really sets in it's going to be rather awkward, as cold showers will be out and it is impossible to get a complete wash in that amount of water. This evening the British put on a short play that had been written by George Williams before he left and which was modelled on the 'Pirates of Penzance'. It was a thundering good show. Twiss, as usual, was magnificent while Gordon Eccles and Pat Brougham were decidedly exciting as voluptuous females!!

Nov 1st   Reveille has been advanced to 0630 as from today but still no word about the wearing of greatcoats. Had our return match with room 22 on the away ground this evening and once again we came out on top in spite of having to put over such words as 'anachronism'.

Nov 2nd   Last night, I managed to buy a drawing book from Freddie Murdock for five packets of Nip cigarettes so this afternoon, feeling very bored with life and having nothing better to do, settled down and managed to reproduce a fair likeness to the old 'benjo' . . . intend to try and get a few more drawings of life in this camp in the future.

Col. Scott came round and warned all the British officers that the Jap 'BBC' were paying us a visit tomorrow and that altho' all officers would be given the opportunity of making a recording to be broadcast to our own people, we were not to do so unless we wanted to get into hot water when we were freed: not that I had any intention of letting Japs use my voice for propaganda purposes.

Nov 3rd   For some unknown reason, the Japs decreed that today was to be a 'Yasume day' (rest day) so we all had a holiday from work and could lie down on our bunks all day long if we so desired . . . the recordings were started today . . .

Nov 4th   Feeling rather out of sorts today so of course I would have to be both on room duty and chicken feeding. This morning I had a bright idea and got George Armstrong to include a message from me to Alec Rattray in his recording to his wife in the hopes that Alec would twig and forward the information on to the folks in case they had not heard about me yet. All that George said was, 'Notify Alec Rattray . . . that A. A. Duncan is OK,' so that there could be no comeback from our authorities.

Neither George nor Atholl knew the effect that the simple coded message would have and they would have to wait well into the next year before they would find out.

Benjo (latrines), Zentsuji, drawn by Captain Duncan, 1943 (see p. 171, 2nd November).

Sketch of East Wing at Zentsuji, drawn by Captain Duncan, 1943.

Nov 5th   *Went out of camp this morning to collect seven sacks of chicken food from a store house on the south side of the town and found the outing very pleasant as the work was not hard – we had the cart along with us – the weather beautifully sunny and mild and the scenery was quite lovely . . .*

Nov 7th–9th   *. . . this evening we have a gramophone recital in our room and a few jazz numbers are being played just now, bring back memories of these happy days before the war when the Saturday evening 'imprompt' was eagerly looked forward to and Elizabeth and I used to spend a few hours enjoying life to its fullest. It's absolutely damnable to think that this war has come along and lifted such a large chunk right out of our lives at a period which is considered to be the best years of one's life. Still, God willing, it should not be too long before we are re-united again . . . I occupied myself by making a blanket pullover . . . and from the centre leaf of my flea bag a balaclava helmet and am very satisfied with the result . . .*

Nov 11th–12th   *There was great jubilation in Zentsuji POW camp this afternoon as one of the chickens laid an egg: when the news was known to the chicken squad, they formed up in a procession with Twiss at the head bearing the precious object on a cushion and then proceeded to make a triumphal journey thro' the camp, several onlookers doing obeisance to it as we passed, and having paraded it before the whole camp, handed it over to the sick bay for consumption. The Japs who witnessed the whole affair are now thoroughly convinced that we are all quite mad!!! . . .*

Also dated 12th November 1943 was the following missive to all Room Leaders from Jim Powell. Atholl copied it out into one of his notebooks so as not to forget the amusement it caused to all concerned:

Circular to all Room Leaders in Zentsuji POW camp
12 November 1943

Gentlemen,

In our capacity as Div. Supply Officer, it is our regrettable duty to notify you of the fact that a diarrhoetic dilemma has occurred, to wit, that there is not now, nor will there be for a month, any supply of bathroom tissue, bung fodder, or, in Zentsuji parlance, benjo paper, for the purpose of excretory eradication.

We assure you that our deepest concern is involved in this matter; however, it is beyond our power to offer you so much as a square inch of the aforementioned material in proof of our bruised feelings.

It has, in view of the inevitable continuances of natural elimination (which are so persistently incognisant of these deplorable circumstances) been recommended that the daily newspaper be utilised for a dual purpose. In this event,

Nature must supercede their diversion to the usual channels outside the camp. Should the paper be put to this use, we must forewarn you that we waive any responsibility for subsequent cases of "pruritis ani" or other complications which may result from contact of tender anal orifices with printers ink. (Printers ink poisoning). Should newspapers be subjected to this use, it is forbidden to use those copies in which pictures of royalty appear. We are sure that you will exercise all possible discretion in this matter.

Gentlemen, until this condition is alleviated, which will not be until next month, it will be futile to question us daily upon this matter, for, tho' a man may be able to talk a chunk of granite out of a quarry, he will not be able to talk a single sheet of 'non-skid' out of Zentsuji.

Until better times, we are, you may be sure, your most sympathetic and heart-broken servants,

Jim Powell 1/Lt, Division 4, Zentsuji, Japan

Nov 13th–14th   *Started to study Maths under Blakey today and hope to be able to polish up my knowledge in this subject in case I go back to complete my degree . . . today eighteen Nip officers came to inspect our quarters so our usual 'Yasume day' was completely spoiled . . .*

Nov 15th   *. . . Maths under Blakey is coming along quite nicely and I am understanding a good deal which I never did before and hope to cover most of the ground for special Maths so that if I do go back and complete my degree, the work won't be too foreign to me.*

Nov 17th   *We got our old blankets withdrawn this afternoon and new ones issued to give us a total of five . . . one of the American officers was caught in the RC storehouse and is now in the 'brig'. Serves him right . . . Pete Kenny came over in the evening and gave us a lecture on the Coastal Command and is going to complete it next week; very interesting lecture indeed . . . Elizabeth's birthday today.*

Nov 18th   *This afternoon after the muster parade Twiss called all the chicken squad into consultation and told us that he had been called up to the office this morning where Hositani had told him that it had been decided that the eggs would be portioned out as follows: – A maximum of 2 per head per month, the balance going to the Jap hospital and bakery, this figure being decided as we only did the manual labour and the Japs had provided every-thing else. He added that if we decided to make an issue of it, all agriculture and rabbit parties would cease as would recreations and that as we would not be working, we would not need so much food so that would be cut down too.*

Nov 19th–21st   *. . . another small issue of sugar and cocoa today and weather now definitely chilly but still we are not allowed to wear greatcoats and of course we have no fires. What it is going to be like in Jan and Feb* *heaven only knows . . . to my mind, one of the good things about this camp is that all the nationalities are mixed up in the various rooms and it is really remarkable just how well we hit it off together . . . Now that winter is upon us, nearly everyone is either sewing, or knitting, this latter being restricted to the lucky few who possess wool and it is amusing to see some great husky male assiduously sewing some small garment, swearing punctuating his stitches . . .*

Nov 22nd–24th *Today about 1,000 letters arrived in camp, presumably off the 'Taia Maru' but from what we hear, they are all for the Americans and the Japs are censoring them at the rate of about thirty a day, taking extracts for propaganda . . . Although I have not been in this godforsaken country for a year yet it seems ages since I left Java and although the days pass quickly enough, the months seem to drag on interminably; when ARE we going to be free again? No news in the papers.*

Nov 25th–28th *Quite a few of the letters have been distributed also some individual parcels which arrived and one lad received a mirror in his parcel which was stamped 'Made in Japan'! . . . I always feel very despondent when mail arrives and there is none for me but the blow is somewhat softened by the fact that the lucky ones frequently let the less fortunate read their letters but naturally that is not the same as getting news yourself. Sandy Robertson, the Aussi doctor, who is suffering from diabetes is in a very bad way as he has come out in a series of ulcers which will not heal and of course, the Japs will do nothing for him and matters have reached such a stage that unless something is done soon we are going to lose him as his mental condition is very bad indeed and he won't eat his food . . . went along to the cricket pitch and passed an hour or so delivering rather wild bowls which were stopped all over the place till one was finally sent over the boundary fence into the magazine grounds, whereupon Jim Addison (RAF) nimbly went over after it and scrambled back again to land at the feet of a rather startled sentry. Nothing said about this.*

Nov 29th *Now that quite a few of the hens are laying we have not only started to ring them but have also christened a few of them and as it fell my lot to name one of them, I called it Joan – wonder what Elizabeth will have to say about this when I tell her?*

Nov 30th *Today another batch of mail came in to the camp but of course there was none for me . . . after supper I got a terrific fit of the blues and it took all of the charm of George Armstrong to snap me out of it . . .*

Dec 1st *. . . à propos of letters, we have received word that we can write a 300 word letter but are not allowed to make any reference to compulsory work, war news, or expectations of release. Tuyn, the Dutchman who was with the APC in Singapore did a profile sketch of me which was really very good. He has done quite a few of them but I think that this is his best effort so far. It's a*

Dr Sandy Robertson, the Australian doctor who suffered from diabetes. He died in camp through neglect.

> *funny thing but since the British refused to broadcast we have had no mail altho' it has been seen up at Tokyo and yet the Americans who did broadcast receive mail regularly.*

The following instructions were found written out in one of the notebooks. This directive was issued as a circular to all POW on 1 December 1943 by the camp authorities:

Circular to POW on Dec 1st 1943

(1) There will be a British Exchange ship leaving Japan in January.

(2) All prisoners of war may now write a letter of approx. 300 words.

(3) Subjects that are NOT to be included are:-

>   (a) War situation
>
>   (b) All references to compulsory work
>
>   (c) Statements such as 'I am convinced I shall be home soon,' and 'I expect to see you soon,' but, 'I hope to see you soon' will be allowed.
>
>   Proverbs or anything that might be in the form of a code will not be allowed.

(4) Owing to the heavy work entailed on the censor at present, any letter that contains references to the above, will just be discarded and the writer will not be allowed another chance to write this mail.

(5) Letters are to be given in as follows:-

>   British to Cmdr Richardson or Lieut Brougham by Dec 4th
>
>   Dutch to Capt Wijs or Capt Oyens by Dec 6th
>
>   Americans to Major Putnam or Cmdr Graf after this date, at the latest by Dec10th.

Put your room number on your letter.

Atholl availed himself of the opportunity and set down a carefully planned and worded letter (see 4th and 18th December for further details). The diary continued:

> Dec 2nd   *I have been elected onto the committee for the room's Xmas celebrations, Schacht, Dalton and Power being the other members and so far we have had quite a few bright ideas . . .*

He was in talented company as Lieutenant Kenneth Schacht, USN (known to one and all as 'Buck') and Lieutenant Norman Power, RN, late of HMS *Exeter* (nicknamed 'Freddie') were both gifted illustrators and cartoonists. The archive contains other fine examples of their work given to him while they were in camp together like this one drawn by Buck Schacht.

'Light Please' drawn by
'Buck' Schacht, USN,
Zentsuji.

December 1943 was fairly uneventful with mail, or rather the lack of it, dominating his thoughts. Christmas planning and one or two amusing incidents helped to lightened the atmosphere:

Dec 3rd   *Capt. Gordon has got a tame pet rabbit which he has named Oliver – after himself – and a common sight is Oliver junior frisking about among the vegetables growing in the garden with Oliver senior following him around! Quite a surprise for us today as three piglets were brought into camp and two more have been promised, this being quite a big step in the right direction . . .*

Dec 4th   *. . . wrote a letter to the folks and sent Dad a power of attorney; hope the Nips will allow this to go through.* (viz 18th December)

This was to be the only letter from him during his captivity that eventually arrived back home. The family received it in July 1944 and confirmed this in their next card, dated 15 July (Elizabeth's card confirming that she also knew of it, followed two weeks later dated 2 August).

Dec 6th   *Quite a few individual parcels arrived in camp and in our room Warren, Stirling, Covington and Kirkpatrick received them, Warren getting some photos of his wife and a watch as well as a lot of food and is about as happy as a dog with two tails; still, I suppose I shall be in a similar state when I get my first news from home but wish that the Japs would get a move on as far as mail for the British community is concerned. Freddie Power has been hard at work of late, turning out Xmas cards etc, and quite apart for the beautiful execution of his art, the ideas are original and very amusing.*

Lieutenant Norman H. (Freddie) Power, RNVR, late HMS *Exeter*.

Gunner Leslie Dursley, RA, taken at Motoyama in 1945.

Dad was to meet up with Freddie again over 44 years later, thanks to my sister Jenny who was instrumental in bringing them together.

In 1989 Jenny, who is a journalist, was working on one of the Chester Chronicle group of newspapers, the *Herald & Post*, a weekly free sheet. During October of that year she serialised Dad's diaries in the paper. Within the first couple of weeks the distribution department was inundated with requests for the paper, so popular had the feature proved to be. Initially it had been intended to run the series for just a month during October. However, in view of the demand she was asked to extend the run and the series covered the twelve weeks up to Christmas. The newspaper came out on a Friday each week. On Monday 4 December, she had not long been at her desk when the telephone rang. A well-spoken gentleman politely asked her if he could please be put through to Captain Duncan, as he wished to speak to him. Intrigued, she asked who it was that was speaking.

'My name is Norman Power. I have just opened a copy of the local newspaper and have come face to face with a photograph of my younger self staring back at me. It was quite a shock!' he said, laughing.

He went on to explain that only a day or so before the newspaper hit his doormat, he had settled into his new home (a flat in Chester) having moved from Lincolnshire only that week. He simply couldn't believe his eyes when he opened the centre spread, to find a photograph of himself.

Jenny was absolutely thrilled and tried hard to retain a professional façade while struggling to control her emotions, knowing exactly what this would mean to Dad. She relished the opportunity to put them in touch with each other and didn't wish to spoil the moment for either of them.

Politely she explained that it wasn't possible for her to give him Captain Duncan's telephone number but, if he would like to leave his details, she would be very happy to pass on the message. As soon as she had hung up she rang Dad, telling him the news as steadily as she could. He was absolutely delighted at the thought of meeting Freddie after so long.

Over the next couple of years they met several times, enjoying each other's company greatly. Dad also received another fine example of Freddie's work to put in his collection (see opposite).

Sadly, the reasons for his move north (to be nearer to his daughter) very soon became evident. Freddie was not a well man and he passed away on 9 February 1992, aged 75.

Freddie wasn't the only contact Dad made through the serialisation. He

"Fred" Power.

LANZAROTE '89
N.H.P.

also heard from one of the men, Leslie Dursley, a gunner who had been in camp in Java and then at Motoyama with him. He was living in Wirral, and when they met up Mr Dursley lent him some photographs taken at Motoyama in 1945 after liberation which Dad had copied (see page 109).

Dad was immensely proud of the serialisation and the interest it generated but the whole business of working through the diary with Jenny, re-living those hateful, frightening days and facing so much of the past, took a heavy toll and for months afterwards he was not himself. He rejoiced in meeting up with old companions, but in so doing they all revisited a place they wished they'd never been to.

Back to December 1943.

Christmas card depicting the three Kings being parachuted in – illustrated and signed by 'Fred' Power and received by Atholl Duncan, December 1989.

Dec 7th . . . Have completed a Xmas card for George Armstrong, depicting a joke he played on his wife when she came to the PI (Philippine Islands) and I think that he should be quite amused by it; at any rate, I know I am . . .

Dec 8th Today, being the second anniversary of the outbreak of the war in the Far East was celebrated by the Nips as a holiday, our Jap Col. delivering an oration to all room leaders, stressing the mighty war results that Japan has obtained etc. Horse shit !!!

The following is the transcript of this oration, once again carefully reproduced in his notebook for posterity:

Address to Prisoners from Japanese Colonel i/c Zentsuji POW Camp

December 8th 1943

'In greeting the second anniversary of the outbreak of the Greater East Asia War, I shall here state a part of my thoughts in wishing the following to be carried out.

By now you must be well aware of the fact, that since the outbreak of the war the Japanese Empire has been obtaining magnificent war results one after the other, especially the recent outstanding achievements in Burma or the several successive brilliant victories being won in the South Sea region, which is unprecedented in the world's annals of war. As time passes on, the firmness of solidarity has been greatly strengthened not only within the Empire, but among all countries of Greater East Asia, while the development and exploitation of raw materials for production necessary for the execution of a long termed war is steadily being progressed by which, I presume, you have conceived the utter invincibility of Japan. After all, as the Anglo-American countries aimlessly increased their most impure and ambiguous ambition which lead us to this war, the Japanese Empire rose in determination, with the sword of justice in her hand, to liberate the one billion people of Greater East Asia. Thus, because of this noble object for war it is only natural and proper that the aforementioned war results were obtained.

You, who are the victims of this ambiguous ambition which caused the war, and who here observe this day of anniversary, undoubtedly have deep emotions within your hearts.

Turning to the state of affairs in the camp, all of you have, in general respectfully observed the various regulations and are endeavouring to display the desired spirit of self discipline, to which I express my respects. Nevertheless, there have been more than a few regrettable cases. For instance, there were several successive cases of punishment inflicted upon those who wrongly conducted themselves, or some who received repeated warnings from the Japanese duty officers and other members of the camp. These are some of the regrettable cases.

Therefore, it is wished that for the sake of the honour of your countries, you should be discreet in your deeds and admonish your fellow prisoners in order to exterminate any repulsive incidents from happening, both during work and in the course of your normal life in camp.

As the second anniversary of the war is here greeted and while the home front is being still more strengthened and the determination to carry out the war is formed anew, I strongly desire that you will further heighten and display the spirit of self discipline. (By this, I end my address).

Col Sugiyama
i/c Zentsuji POW Camp

Dec 9th . . . *Sandy Robertson has been turfed out of the sickbay on orders from the Jap doctor – no reason being given for this.*

Dec 10th *Strang, one of the Americans in Room 19 who is in the publishing business is trying to collect material for a souvenir book to be published when we get out of here, the idea being to collect the story of each phase of the campaigns and subsequent POW camps and lead up to the life here in Zentsuji; poems, sketches and articles all to be included as well as a rogues gallery; I think this is a very good idea and hope that something comes of it.*

Dec 12th . . . *quite busy of late cutting out and colouring ornaments for our room Xmas tree and think that we are going to have quite a creditable show on the 25th: there's one thing, I'm pretty sure that next year at this time, I shall be far from both Zentsuji and Japan.*

Dec 13th–16th . . . *about 5,700 letters have arrived in camp but I am not expecting any, and am more or less resigned to being without any mail during my captivity: one thing that has struck me about most of the individual parcels that have been arriving of late for the Americans is the shoddy junk which is put in them, cotton socks and singlets, cheaply woven towels and a varying assortment of cheap confectionery. Nor is this opinion based on an acute dose of sour grapes for I really do not envy anyone such stuff: I know I should be pretty annoyed if I received a parcel from home which contained no woollen goods . . . Twiss interviewed the Allied POW committee to try and get them to do something about the egg problem but could get no satisfaction out of them at all, as they were all in favour of adopting a laissez-faire attitude...by the way permission was given for greatcoats to be worn any time except on roll calls – just the time when we need them most !!!*

Dec 18th . . . *with reference to the 5,700 letters which arrived in camp recently, these were all ready for distribution when the local civilian gestapo descended on the camp and took them all away to re-censor them just to check up and see that the censors in the camp were doing their job. We were called over to the office today to sign our outgoing mail, my power of attorney being accepted with no questions asked.* [It arrived in Scotland in July 1944 and his father lodged it with a local solicitor for safe keeping – see 1st and 4th December for further explanation.]

Dec 19th . . . *I am reading quite an interesting book just now, the title being 'Out of the Night', which deals with the experiences of a communist before and after he was caught by the Gestapo: certainly it's grim reading...*

Dec 21st *Col. Hazel received a letter today so as he has been in my prison group from the start, there is a chance that I might receive one . . . this morning Joe Dalton, Lasher and I went down behind the hen house and made evergreen wreaths to hang up in the windows as Xmas decorations.*

Captain Joseph Kwiatkowski, 60th CA (AA) US Army.

We have got a short radio-travel skit which we are going to put on after breakfast on Xmas day and I think – and hope – that it should go down quite well.

Dec 22nd   Very little doing all day, the only note-worthy event being that Joe Kwiatkowski managed to get some paper streamers which saved the day as far as our Christmas decorations were concerned as . . . apart from a rather futuristic Santa Claus on a sled with very saucy reindeer and some evergreen, surreptitiously removed from the young trees in the camp, we had nothing with which to relieve the grim and drab aspect of our room . . .

Dec 23rd   Busy all day getting the room ready for Xmas, and have really achieved quite remarkable results considering the materials we had to work with. The Japs provided us with some coloured paper and this was cut into streamers and put quite a cheery air to the rather forbidding usual aspect of the room.

The Prisoner's Alphabet written by Lieutenant Colonel E. J. Hazel.

The Prisoner's Alphabet.

A is the Army who'd never give up,
B is the British part sold for a pup,
C's Capitulation which forced us to face
D which is Dysentery, Dirt, and Disgrace.
E's the eruptions under our skins,
F's the Fatigue we must do for our sins,
G is for Guilder, – not paid so we owe it,
H is for Hazel, this doggerel poet.
I is for Idoh who loved to give slaps,
J is for Java and Johnstone and Japs.
K is the Kitchen which boils up our scum,
L's the Latrine much frequented by some.
M is our menu, – Rice, Rice, Rice or Rice,
N is for Nipponese Not Nearly Nice,
O is the Orient where we remain,
P is for Priok, Prison, and Pain,
Q's for our Quislings so loathsome to see,
R is for Rations and R.A.S.C.
S is their stomachs most strangely distended,
T is the Tinned Meat most starngely expended,
U is for Us, Unhappy, Unfed,
V is our Victory, not far ahead.
W's the Weevils they give us to eat,
x the amount of a prisoner's meat,
Y is the Yes-Man, a scandal and blight,
and Z is our Zeal to be back in the fight.

E.J.Hazel, Lt.-Col.

Dec 24th   *Spent a very busy and tiring day putting the finishing touches to everything – Joe Kwiatkowski has made a nativity scene which we have decorated with evergreen and 'snow' (Nip toothpowder) and the small Christmas tree has been covered with 'Fougasse' figures cut out from paper and coloured. When the Jap Col. inspected each room he was quite tickled with the whole show. In the evening we had a concert of Xmas carols, which were beautifully sung by the massed choirs and on listening to this my thoughts went straight back to home and as I write this my mind is not on the job as I have not come back to earth yet. . . .*

Dec 25th   *Without exception today has been the best day I have spent, as yet, as a POW. Immediately after morning roll call, the room Xmas committee got busy and prepared our half of the room for our party: our bay was screened off by blankets, the tables were covered with sheets, paper doilies were provided for the plates, imitation candles and paper streamers providing the table decorations along with the place cards. Just after the meal had begun, old Tom came in, dressed up as Santa Claus and distributed the presents to each member. When the meal had finished the radio travelogue skit was put on, the highlight of this being Lasher's Indian war dance which was interrupted by the arrival of the guard commander who was more than startled to see a paint be-daubed face peering at him round the door and a hand brandishing an exceedingly murderous-looking cleaver just above it. After breakfast I went round and extended the season's greeting to my various friends – consuming innumerable cups of tea etc, en route – the galley was supplying hot water all day – and ended up at the chicken house only to find the place swarming with Nips armed with a movie camera bent on getting propaganda pictures, so beat a hasty retreat before I got roped in for something.*

During the afternoon the Division party was held in rooms 21 and 22 but to my mind this fell rather short of the mark as there was no community singing – something I had hoped for – but the singing of the various national anthems – British, American and Dutch was beautifully rendered by the choir. In the evening there was a performance of Dickens' 'Christmas Carol' which was very polished and which brought to a close a highly successful and enjoyable day. The food all day was excellent, M & V stew, rice (and for Dutch, Mac and myself porridge), currant hotchpotch for breakfast with cocoa for a beverage; rabbit and chicken stew and rice and bread for lunch, bully stew and sweet cakes and rice for supper as well as currant pie.

As we were issued with 2 RC boxes per three men on the previous evening there was no lack of good cheer and some people managed to bribe the guards to get them Jap whisky @ Y400 per bottle.

A great deal of ingenuity was displayed in some of the Christmas cards and decorations and several rooms held a display of their cards so that all who so

Christmas card to Atholl drawn by George Armstrong, December 1943. Note the chicken on top of the engine – called Joan! (see page 175 – 29 November).

wished could come round and inspect them; there were two very minor incidents during the course of the day, the first being that the Japs permitted a party to go to the cemetery to hold a short service over the graves there but then asked for a repeat performance so that they could make a film of it and did not like it when several of the party refused. The other occurred inside the camp when the ball that some of the lads were playing with went over the camp fence. One lad made as if to climb on the fence and ask a Nip on the other side to pass it back when Asabuki saw him, called him over and said, 'People in your country have been shot for that; it would be a great pity if we had to shoot you, especially on Xmas day!!!'

Dec 26th   Much to my surprise – and relief there has been no repercussions for our yesterday's feasting, although some of the people have not been so lucky as I have – as the benjo indicated this morning!!! Room 19 held their Xmas party at lunchtime today and put on an excellent show, having manufactured a large cake out of eggs, rice, milk, cocoa, prunes, raisins and plum jam, the icing being made from beaten up eggs, butter and milk, whilst the decorations round the sides and top were formed from tangerine leaves. Just when their party had got under way a deputation from our room went in, greeted them, and then 'Dutch' after a suitable speech presented them with a benjo bottle amidst roars of applause and laughter. This evening in the canteen there was a performance of 'Ali Baba' which was without exception the funniest show we have had yet, as contrary to Jap orders, costumes were used and Hutch-Smith, Irwin and Pat Brougham dressed up as robbers were absolute masterpieces; Gordon Eccles as an usherette created quite a stir too.

Dec 27th   Very little doing all day. Started jotting down the sub headings for the story about Java which I am to write for Strang's book. Rumour has it that we are going to be allowed to write another card which will go out on the exchange ship and this seems to be quite feasible.

Dec 28th   . . . got a new strap and glass fitted to my watch, these repairs being done in the course of one day – which is quite good service to be given to a POW!! The Nip doctor has now ordered Sandy Robertson to appear on morning tenko despite the fact that he is still a very sick man, and will not even bother to visit him, let alone treat him.

Dec 29th   . . . I have been very surprised and rather disgusted at some of the habits of various people in this camp and one thing which particularly revolts me is the open mouthed mastication of chewing gum as well as the practice of sticking the discarded residue of this on the under side of tables etc. Another very pernicious habit is that of spitting and hoicking, this last driving me almost into a frenzy.

Dec 30th   . . . *quite a few more parcels came into camp today for the Americans, being forwarded from Osaka camp so perhaps some day soon I may get some mail. Managed to buy some notebooks thro' the black market, the price being Y10 – Y15 each. It's a hell of a price to pay for a 30ct book but it is the only way I can get hold of paper to get another diary bound for the new year.*

Dec 31st   *Well, this is the last day of the year of our Lord 1943 and looking back it has not been too bad from practically every aspect considering the fact that I am a POW. One interesting feature has been the gradual change of the tone of the Jap press from one of bombast to that of acute anxiety about everything pertaining to this war and there is little doubt in my mind that the end of it all will come during the next year, the first step in this being the collapse of the European show which, I imagine, should come about the late spring or early summer and that will be quickly followed by Japan's exit from the war as she cannot hope to hold out against the combined might of the Allies. For one thing, they are not only short of war materials as can be seen from the articles which appear practically daily in the papers but also there is an acute shortage of all types of civilian commodities, coal, food and paper being some that we have noticed inside this camp. A few weeks ago, our committee asked the Jap Col. about mail for the British and also requested that the distribution of Red Cross supplies should be put in our hands but no reply was received about this until today when it was announced that as the Jap govt was responsible for their collection and distribution the request could not be granted, but "Sake Pete" was there to manage such matters and would always listen to suggestions, and as regards the former, there were lots of letters up at Tokyo for us, but they were either so badly written or addressed that it took the censors a long time to decipher and sort them out!!!*

Just how much longer would they have to wait until they received news from home?

Postscript: Not the End, Just Another Beginning

Both in December 1942 and again in December 1943, Captain Duncan finished the last day of the year on a reflective note. Not unusual perhaps, as that is what a year end tends to provoke. However, despite being anything but 'normal' years, he still needed to mark them. Regardless of the misery and discomforts of his situation, his natural instinct was to acknowledge the occasion – it helped.

Years later, when my sisters and I were growing up, my parents held annual New Year's Eve fancy dress parties. These occasions became legendary among their circle of friends. Mum put on a splendid feast: beef, ham, turkey and of course, haggis with 'tatties' and 'neeps', accompanied by as many different salads as there were helpers. It took all her time and energy to organise. Dad meanwhile, aided and abetted by several close friends, reverted to boyhood and transformed the large open hallway in the centre of the house into a 'den'. Whatever theme they came up with, Hillbillies and Flower Power coming readily to my mind, the den was dressed accordingly. In the case of the former, the hallway had a shack with veranda built against the lounge wall while the latter produced a floral feast, the hall bedecked with hundreds of plastic flowers, courtesy of a patient who was a florist!

It strikes me that there is a link here: the need to mark this occasion was for him, so special. Throughout his captivity the one thing that he hung on to was a determination to survive. His diaries show many reasons for this: he would have to provide for Elizabeth as they were going to be married; the need to keep up with his studies to gain his degree once back at home. There were holidays he was going to take, books he must read, restaurants he would like to dine in . . . There are so many lists in his notebooks which bear testament to his determined spirit and will to live. He didn't give up. Thoughts of escape were still on his mind despite having been a prisoner for over a year and the impossibility of such action in reality. Nevertheless, in March 1943 he went so far as to write in his diary about an idea for escape.

The last day of 1943 was not for Atholl an ending; it marked the beginning of a new year. Even though he had no way of knowing how long he would remain in captivity, or what hardships lay ahead, 1944 held hope for his liberation, for better conditions, for more food, and above all, for contact with his loved ones . . .

Unbeknown to him, it was only to be a matter of days before his family and Elizabeth would be overjoyed and reassured by the arrival, first by cable and later by letter, of Lieutenant George Armstrong's coded message which had been recorded in November 1943. The postcard below arrived at Alec Rattray's home in San José, along with dozens of others, on 9 January 1944. They were heralded by a constantly ringing telephone, with callers repeating the same message that they had heard during a radio broadcast from Tokyo:

'. . . *Notify Alec Rattray, 2111 Lincoln Avenue, San José, California, that A. A. Duncan is OK . . .*'

Alec immediately contacted St Andrews with the news contained in the message. This turned out to be the first communication directly from Atholl (albeit via his friend). Finally, they had word from him: now they knew that he was still alive. Their prayers had been answered, there was still hope.

Imagine the joy that one sentence must have brought to them all. For Elizabeth and the family at least, the waiting was over; Atholl would have to wait a while longer, but very soon both he and they could begin to contemplate the possibility of starting to share life once again.

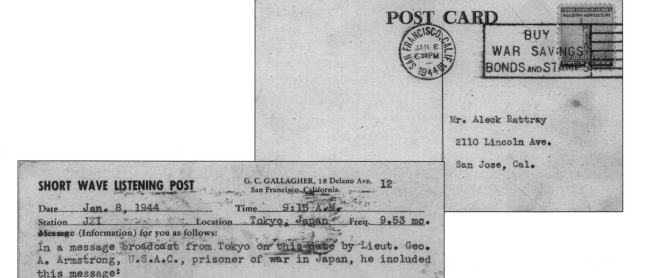

Appendix
List of prisoners of war known to Captain Duncan

Some of these names appear in the text of his diaries and in this book (see Index). A number do not appear in this book but will be mentioned in the sequel which will cover the years 1944–1946. Other names appear in one of four separate lists of personnel that Captain Duncan kept in different notebooks. A number of entries are handwritten by the individuals concerned, and for the purposes of illustration I have reproduced sample pages of one of these notebooks.

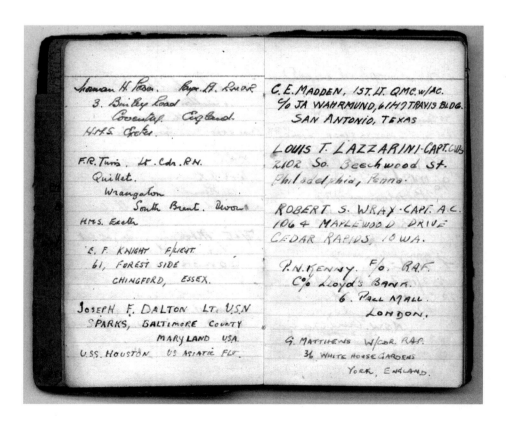

Adair, William G, Capt, Inf US Army

Addison, James, F/Lt, RAF

Armstrong, George H, 1/Lt USAC 17th
Pursuit Sqdn

Baldwin, James H, 2/Lt, QMC US Army

Balfour, W (Bill) M, Lt, RE

Barnley, Sqn/Ldr

Bassett

Bathgate, W H, Capt, AIF

Beadnall, Dr

Berkeley, Dr A

Besbeck, Louis B, Capt, Inf US Army

Bird, P/Officer, RAFVR

Bishop, E R, F/O 60953, RAF

Black, R B, Capt, RA Colonial Admin
Service

Blaikie

Blakey, George W, Capt, 77th AAA, RA

Blanchard, W T (Bob), Sqn/Ldr

Boggs, Kenneth L, Capt, US Army

Bowden, W E, Fl/Lt, RAF 60 Sqd

Bridges, Dr A

Brooke-Popham, Sir Robert, Air Chief
Marshal, C-in-C

Brookham, see Brooke-Popham above

Brooks, Lee C, Capt, 45th Inf US Army

Brougham, P, Lt, RN

Bruce, Alex R, Lt, RE

Bruce, William, Capt, 2/Btn A&SH

Buchanan, B McD, Lt, RE

Bucke, C.E. (Pip) Lt, RC Signals

Burr, Duncan Lt, 6th Btn Victorian
Scottish

Bussel, G John, Lt, AIF

Caldicot, G H, Lt, RE

Campbell, Keith, Capt, 6th (Hey) Regt, RA

Campbell, Major

Campion, Des F, Lt A&SH

Carter, William W, Lt, RA

Cassidy, Sgt

Chandler, A A, Lt, RAE

Chinn, Gordon W, Lt, AIF

Clarke, Alfe, Lt, AIF

Connibear, Robin J M, Lt, RNVR

Cooper, S H, Lt, RAA

Covington, James M, Capt, QMC

Cowling, John H, Ch Skip, RNR

Crane, Russell H, Lt, AIF

Cutbush, Major

Dalton, Joseph F, Lt, US Navy

Dant, Alan

Day, Steven V.B. 2/Lt Courier & Pioneers

Dobbin, Lt Colonel, G2 JASO

Dowse, H E W (Pat), Lt, 2/22 Btn, AIF

Dukes

Dunlop, Nigel N H, Sqn/Ldr 41269, RAF

Dursley, Leslie, Gunner RA (869121)

Earle, Major

Eccles, Gordon

Emmett, B R, Major RA

Erwin, H S, Lt, 2/22 Btn, AIF

Espie, W N, Lt, RE

Exley

Field, Brian E, Lt

Frow, W/Cmdr

Glasgow, Dennis P G, Lt

Godfrey, The Reverend Rupert C R,
Padre (Tandjong Priok)

Gordon, Oliver, Capt, HMS Exeter, RN

Grant, W Gordon, Lt, 2/22 Btn, AIF

Grant, W R, Ch Eng

Gregg, Donald G, Capt, Inf US Army

Hamilton, C A, Capt, RE

Harper, John

Harper-Holdcroft, The Reverend R H,
Padre (Tandjong Priok)

Hay, John, Capt, US Army

Hazel, E H, Colonel

Hepburn, J, Capt, 2/20 Btn, AIF

Hiley, Eric V, Lt, 2/15 Fd RAA, AIF

Hill, Graham, Lt, Mddx Regt

Hill, Ralph O, 1/Lt, 60th CA AA

Humble, M, Lt US Army

Hunt, 2/Lt

Hutcheson, F/Lt, RAF

Hutchinson-Smith, D C, Capt, AIF

Jackson, C H, Capt, Johore Military Force

Jaeger, Fred

Jameson, CSM

Jordan, R, Major, RASC

Keefe, Pat, AC1

Kenny, Peter N, F/O, RAF

Kimber

King, John (Jock) C R, Lt, RE

Kinnear, Duncan G R, Sub-Lt, RNR

Kirkpatrick

Knight, E Frank, F/Lt, RAF

Knowles, Jack

Kuhns, Clinton W (Pappy), Capt, Inf US Army

Kwiatkowski, Joseph (Joe) D, Capt, 60th CA AA

Lambert, Dr John

Lasher, Erwin W, Capt, Inf US Army

Lazzarini, Louis T Capt, CWS

Lord, Robert (Bob) G, Lt, AIF

Maclean, Angus D, Capt, A&SH Gen list

Madden, C Ed, 1/Lt, QMC W/AC

Magee III, Thomas, Lt, USNR

Mainprice, M G, F/Lt, RAAF

Martin, Private Allan

Matthews, G, W/Cmder, RAF (SBO Ube)

Maxfield

Millan

Montgomery-Campbell, Derrick G, Lt, 2/A&SH

Morris, Angus M, P/O

Morrison, Jim, RAF

Morton, Hugh, Lt, RNR

Moulden, D, Sqdn/Ldr, RAF

Murdoch, Freddie

Murray, A E (Buster), Lt

Nichol, G J, Lt, 6th Btn Victorian Scottish

O'Neil, Paddy, Bombadier

Owen, Lt Commander

Oyens, C W A (Bruce) Captain, Dutch IAF

Payne, Lt, USNAC

Pearson, Brigadier, I/C16th AA Bde HQ

Petrie, R R, Lt Col, OC RASC (SBO Motoyama)

Phillips, The Reverend, Padre (Tandjong Priok)

Pitt, Joshua (Jock), Lt, AIF

Plunkett, W R

Porter, Felix N, Capt, Inf US Army

Power, N H (Freddie), Lt, Paymaster RNVR

Quist

Richardson, H D, Commander, RN – (SBO Zentsuji)

Roberts, L

Robertson, A (Sandy), Dr

Robertson, K R, Lt, RAA

Rogge, Warren O

Russell, Lt Colonel, AQMG

Ryan

Ryder, John F, Lt, US Navy

Saunders, Colonel

Schacht, Kenneth T (Buck), Lt, US Navy

Scott, Lt Colonel

Scott, C W, Lt, RA

Simpson, J E

Sitwell, Major General

Smith, George E, Pte, A&SH (Batman)

Smith, John H, Lt, A&SH

Stacy, Brian P, F/Lt, RAAF

Stirling, Warren C, Capt, US Army AC

Strang

Stuart, Lt Colonel, Mddx Regt

Swartout, R, Lt, USNR

Thompson, M W, Capt, RASC

Tooley, A C, Lt

Trillwood, F/Officer, RAF

Tuyn, M C, 1/Lieutenant

Twiss, Frank R, Lt Cmdr, RN

Vandervoord, Private, (Dutch)

Van Peenan, Dr Hubert J, Lt/Cdr, USN

Walker, Private

Warren

Webber, Paul St C, Lt, RC Sigs

Webber, Richard (Dick), Lt

West-Watson, E C W, Lt

Whiting, Major, OC 2nd Echelon (SBO Tandjong Priok)

Whitty, A.E., Lieutenant RA

Wickham, J H D, Lt

Williams Fulford, H C R, Colonial Admin Service

Williams, George - press/broadcasting

Wilson, Alex R, P/O, RAF

Wray, Robert S, Capt, USAC

Young, Bombadier

Bibliography

Baxter, F. John, *Not Much of a Picnic,* F. J. Baxter, 1995.

Blair, John S. G., *History of St Andrews OTC,* Scottish Academic Press, 1982.

Fletcher-Cooke, Sir John, *The Emperor's Guest,* Hutchinson of London, 1971.

McCormick, Audrey Holmes & Jonathan Moffatt, *Moon over Malaya,* Coombe Publishing, 1999.

Mitchell, R. Keith, *42 Months in Durance Vile,* Robert Hale, 1997.

Stewart, Brigadier I. MacA, DSO, OBE, MC, *History of the 2nd Argylls, Malayan Campaign 1941–42,* Thomas Nelson & Sons Ltd, 1947.

The Straits Times Annual 1941.

Periodicals

LIFE Magazine, 21 July 1941, Life Publications.

The Nippon Times, 23 June 1943, Japanese Government.

The Straits Times Annual 1941, Straits Times Newspapers, Singapore.

Internet:

COFEPOW   www.cofepow.co.uk
(Children and Families of Far Eastern Prisoners of War)

Imperial War Museum   www.iwm.org.uk

Royal British Legion   www.britishlegion.org.uk

British Red Cross   www.redcross.org.uk

NEXPOWA   www.prisonerofwar.freeservers.com
(National Ex-Prisoners of War Association, UK)

Scots at War   www.saw.arts.ed.ac.uk

American Ex-POW Association   www.axpow.org

Index